£25

GW00985516

Ballyknockan: A Wicklow Stonecutters' Village

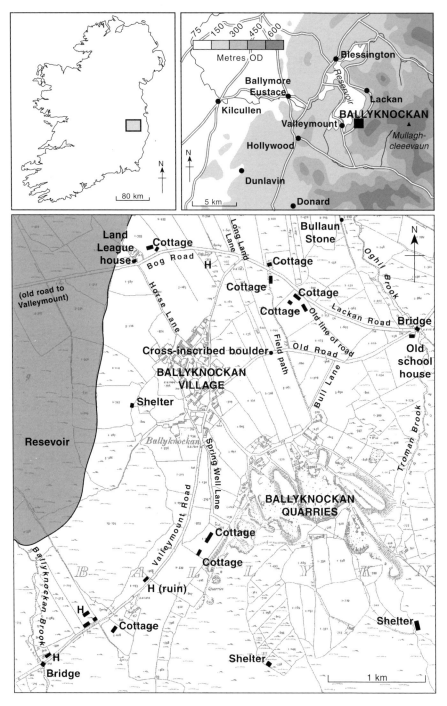

Ballyknockan: The village and its location by Matthew Stout (based on the Ordnance Survey by permission of the Government, Permit No. 6529)

Ballyknockan
A Wicklow Stonecutters' Village

Séamas Ó Maitiú

AND

Barry O'Reilly

With a Foreword by

Dr Maurice Craig

The Woodfield Press

This book was typeset in Ireland by
Gough Typesetting Services for
THE WOODFIELD PRESS
17 Jamestown Square, Inchicore,
Dublin 8, Ireland.

© The Woodfield Press 1997.

A catalogue record for this title
is available from the British Library.

ISBN 0-9528453-5-0

IMPORTANT NOTICE

The quarries at Ballyknockan are potentially very hazardous places. Access to them or to any building, feature or location mentioned in this book should not be assumed.

Printed in Ireland by
Genprint Ltd

Contents

THE COMMUNITY

THE VILLAGE

List of Illustrations

Foreword

Ballyknockan is unique among the villages of Leinster, perhaps unique in all Ireland. It must always have been surprising and delightful to find it, tucked away on the North-West edge of the Wicklow massif. If it was remote when first settled, it is, in a sense, even more remote now, since the formation of the Blessington lake has made the approach, along the contour above the shore, more scenically romantic. And the moment you come on it, you realise that stone is the whole of its being. Ballyknockan is there because of stone, and almost everything in sight is made of stone, even things which in other villages are made of less durable materials. Everywhere there is evidence that though the lives of the quarrymen must have been hard and sometimes dangerous, they could not help playing with stone, after hours, so to speak, just for the fun of the thing.

Building in stone has such a long history in Ireland that it comes as a surprise to learn that the history of Ballyknockan goes back for less than two centuries. As Barry O'Reilly and Séamas Ó Maitiú record, the quarry did not start till 1824. But the tradition is much older, almost as old as human life on this island. Traditionally, masons in the Middle Ages moved about, following opportunities at work, so that the Duffys and others who came to Ballyknockan from 1824 onwards brought with them a well-established capital of craft, experience and skill.

As the authors make clear, it was not just a matter of extracting the stone from the hillside, even of squaring it up into useable shapes and sizes. In some cases at least, the final shape, even of elaborately carved architectural components, was put on it before it left the quarry. So, for one reason or another, odd carved features, intended for distant locations, may still be seen lying about here and there. Years ago I remember seeing a massive Ionic capital, which I photographed, in the grass beside a lane. I was told that it had been intended for the Mater Hospital in Dublin but was found to be flawed. Where is it now? Gracing somebody's garden, I expect. But the lion is still there: roughed out but found, too late, to be not quite large enough for the specification. Long may he remain to delight the casual visitor.

That visitor will find his enjoyment and understanding of Ballyknockan is greatly enhanced by this book, which covers, in a short span, every aspect of life and work in this remarkable and memorable place.

Dr Maurice Craig

Glossary

Ashlar	Stonework in a wall which is well-faced and stones are hewn into regular blocks, finely faced and fitted tightly together giving a very formal effect.
Barge	The top stones of a gable wall.
Capital	The top (usually decorated) of a column.
Chamfered	Where the corner block of stone or a building has been bevelled or 'cut off' at an angle of 45 degrees.
Column	A vertical pillar, usually round in plan and which supports the porch or portico of large, formal and public buildings.
Direct-entry	House layout where the front door and the hearth are located at opposite ends of the kitchen.
Finial	A decorative top to a gable or porch.
Gabled (roof)	Having two roof slopes or surfaces.
Hearth	The main fireplace in a traditional kitchen.
Hipped (roof)	Having four roof slopes or surfaces.
Jamb	The vertical side of a window, doorway or fireplace.
Lintel	The piece of stone or timber spanning a door or window opening and which carries the weight of the walling above.
Lobby-entry	House layout where a lobby or hall is formed between the front door of the house and a wall protecting from the hearth wall, screening the fire from draughts.
Sill	The bottom of a window.
Verge	The edge of a sloping roof which overhangs a gable wall.
Vernacular	Architecture without an architect. Buildings designed and erected by their owners, employing locally-acquired materials, traditional skills and drawing upon inspiration handed down orally and by example.

Introduction

THE LOCATION

The townland of Ballyknockan is bounded by the Poulaphuca Reservoir to the west and north, Oghill Brook to the north-east, the Ballyknockan Brook to the south-west and Moanbane Mountain to the south and south-east.

The whole region, located on the western edge of the Wicklow Massif, is dominated by the Poulaphuca Reservoir (often called 'Blessington Lakes'), fed by the Liffey and King's Rivers. Moanbane (703m high) overlooks the village from the east. Small gaps in the almost completely mountainous vista allow glimpses of Ballymore Eustace (8 km WSW) and the district's main settlement, Blessington (7 km NNW). The flooding of the district in 1940, to a height of 180 m/500 ft a.s.l. resulted in the formation of several large areas of water, totalling c. 20 sq. km. Valleymount, 2 km due west of Ballyknockan, became a peninsula between two expanses of water. The trauma caused by the flooding of the district is still alive today and has been recounted in the book *Memories of the Liffey Valley* (Griffin 1992).

THE UNIQUENESS OF THE PLACE

Signs on the approach roads welcome visitors to 'Ballyknockan Granite Village' and helps prepare them for a most remarkable heritage. The basic form of the buildings is not remarkable from a national vernacular architectural standpoint. It is rather the excellence of their construction and the quality of architectural detailing that lifts the village out of the ordinary. In this they are perhaps unique in Ireland.

Door and window surrounds, chimneys, fireplaces, verges and barges are almost always well-cut and dressed and often chamfered. Associated outbuildings are similarly treated. Ashlar work is common in the village. Only wells, drains and structures built into the slope tend to be rougher in construction. Floors are often of well-fitted stone flags. Fireplaces tend to be decorated, albeit soberly. Worked stone intended for buildings and carved decorative pieces for churches, graveyards, etc. lie scattered throughout the district.

In recognition of its cultural importance, the whole village is listed in the Wicklow County Development Plan. An appropriate response to safeguarding the heritage of Ballyknockan is required. This will involve careful consideration of any infill development and buildings on the approach roads.

A **survey** of the architecture of the village was facilitated by grant aid
from the Royal Irish Academy.

ACKNOWLEDGMENTS

We would like to thank the people of Ballyknockan for sharing the lore of
their community's past with us and in which they have an obvious pride. A
special thanks goes to Rosie O'Reilly, Mary McEvoy, Christy and Billy McEvoy
(The Brook), Maura, Dan and Pat Cullen, Pat Foster, Teresa and Dónall
McEvoy, Michael Freeman, John Brady (Newtown, Donard), Andy Farrington,
Christy Foster, Fr. R. Cantwell, Valleymount who has done so much to
stimulate interest in the history of his parish, Maria Brosnan, Patrick Wise-
Jackson, T.C.D., Seán and Kathleen O'Sullivan, Mary Deevy, Joe Fenwick,
Margareth Keane, Seán Kirwin, Dave Moore, Hilary Opie, Aidan O'Sullivan,
Helen Harnett, Dr Matthew Stout, Dr Maurice Craig, The Royal Irish Academy, and our patient spouses Gráinne Uí Maitiú and Jean Farrelly.

Financial assistance from the Creedon Group Ltd enabled us to provide
the fine colour cover, for which many thanks.

Line drawings by Margaret Keane. Maps and plans prepared by Matthew Stout.

Exerpts from *In Monavalla* by Joseph Brady (Dublin 1963) by kind permission of the publishers.

Séamas Ó Maitiú and *Barry O'Reilly*

THE COMMUNITY

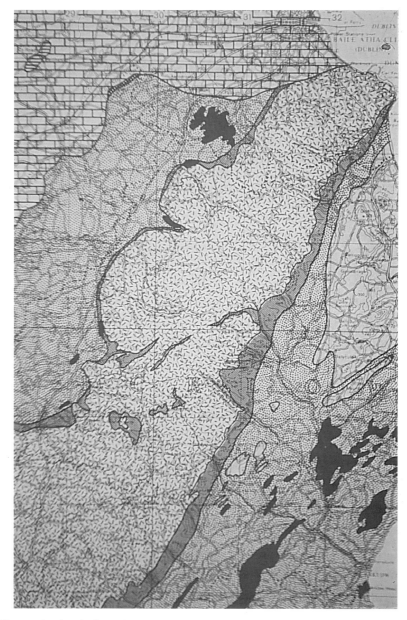

The massive band of granite running south west from Dublin bay to County Carlow.
Ballyknoakan lies on its westerly fringe.

The birth of a tradition

'Paul Duffy was the first man to raise the hammer in Ballyknockan', so says Rosie O'Reilly, the village's best-known oral historian, and while various stonecutting families will give you different dates at which their ancestors started the craft there, the earliest documentary record extant ascribes the opening of large-scale quarrying in Ballyknockan to the year 1824.

The townland and village of Ballyknockan lies on the western fringe of the Wicklow Mountains and close to the western edge of the massive band of granite which extends from the south county Dublin coast in a south westerly direction to County Carlow. In 1838 the Ordnance Survey field workers who moved through the country in preparation for the first ordnance maps visited Ballyknockan and recorded that the granite quarry there was 'the best in this part of the kingdom and has been in use for the last 14 years'. In 1838 they noted there were 160 men employed there.

Stone cutting is a craft that does not just spring up out of the ground on the discovery of a promising seam of rock. It is passed on from generation to generation and stonecutters have always been willing to follow their trade. The question arises then as to where the craft of stonecutting came to Ballyknockan from? The people of Ballyknockan are in no doubt as to this; they will tell you that the first stonecutters came to their area from Golden Hill, Manor Kilbride, and the earliest history of granite-quarrying and stone-cutting in west Wicklow is to be found there.

Golden Hill is a long low brow in the parish of Kilbride not far from the Dublin border. In the building boom of the eighteenth century which resulted in what we know as Georgian Dublin many of the public edifices were constructed of Golden Hill granite. These include the Custom House, the Four Courts, many of the buildings in Trinity College and Nelson's Pillar in 1808 and the General Post Office, opened ten years later. The most substantial building built locally from Golden Hill granite was Russborough, erected by the Leeson family in the 1740s

On Jacob Neville's map of Wicklow, dated 1760, Golden Hill 'freestone quarry' is clearly marked together with another quarry at Oldcourt some one and a half miles away. This map does not show any quarry at Ballyknockan nor indeed any road to it. A comment on a map and short description of Ballyknockan made for the Cobbe family, who owned the townland in 1777, shows no sign of a quarry and states that 'the road throe this farm and the

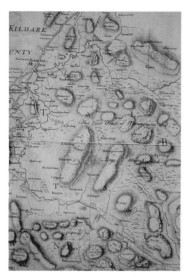

Part of Jacob Neville's map of Wicklow 1760. While 'freestone quarries' are noted at Golden Hill and Oldcourt, there is no sign of quarrying at Ballyknockan

former (the neighbouring townland of Ballinastockan) should be presented and made passable for cars which at present only back loads can pass except to Lacken from which is a tolerable road to Blessington'. It would have been impractical to carry stone by packhorse so commercial quarrying would have to await better communications. An updated map of Wicklow by Jacob Neville's brother, A.R. Neville, which was surveyed in 1798 of all years, still does not show any quarry in Ballyknockan. The cartouches on these maps show quarrying and mining activity and the transport of stone elsewhere in Wicklow.

From all this there appears no reason to doubt the Ordnance Survey field workers when they place the opening of a quarry in Ballyknockan in the early 1820s. It is probable that stoneworkers came to it when better road communications opened it up and when the supply of stone at Golden Hill and Oldcourt deteriorated. And so this

Cartouche from Jacob Neville's map of Wiclow 1760 shows early mining and quarrying activity

brings us back again to Paul Duffy. According to a tradition in Rosie O'Reilly's family it was a Sunday when Paul Duffy and Patrick Olligan came on a back to back trap to survey the potential for stone in Ballyknockan. On the completion of their investigations Olligan remarked to Duffy that there was a great future for granite in Ballyknockan, and how right he was.

Apart from the obvious potential of an almost endless supply of superior stone another reason why Ballyknockan was looked at may have been the fact that both the land of Golden Hill and Ballyknockan belonged to the one landlord. The Cobbe, later the Joy family, owned separately land in Kilbride and a stretch of land between Lacken and Ballyknockan and may have been instrumental in developing Ballyknockan when Golden Hill became depleted.

It is known that Olligan or Holligan – later Halligan – was quarrying in Golden Hill when that quarry was in its heyday. In the book *In Monavalla*, a fictionalised autobiography by Fr Maurice Browne, a curate in the parish of Blackditches or Valleymount, under the pen-name Joseph Brady, the author says that Olligan bought land in Ballyknockan from a Foster of Ballyknockan for £10 in order to supply stone for the building of Russborough. Due to the facts stated above this is highly unlikely and the stone used in Russborough is reckoned to be from Golden Hill. Fr Browne goes on to say that many of the stonecutters, up to 400, then went to Ballyknockan from Golden Hill to supply stone for the Kingsbridge station in 1815. This of course could not be accurate because no railway was built in Ireland until 1834.

He says that they kept their houses in Kilbride and would leave before daybreak on a Monday morning to walk to Ballyknockan to work at six o'clock. They had an hour's break at mid-day and did not stop working again until they heard the Angelus bell rining in Valleymount. They lodged in Ballyknockan during the week and left again for Kilbride on Saturday afternoon. The ringing of the Angelus bell in the valley announcing the end of the working day is often spoken of. It is said that one greedy quarry-owner asked the priest to cease the practise but was, not surprisingly, sent packing. The name Olligan crops up again in both Kilbride and Ballyknockan and Fr Browne's story probably does embody some memory of a large influx of workers from Kilbride.

The pre-quarry townland was similar to many of the townlands on the western fringes of the mountains where the rundale system prevailed. A small cluster of dwelllings, a clachan, was surrounded by its enclosed infields and open outfields. There was a string of such clusters along the fringe of the hills, Lacken and Ballinastockan being other examples. The Cobbe estate map gives us a picture of landholding in the townland before the advent of quarrying. The townland was divided into two, the north quarter and the south quarter; it is probably that there were also east and west quarters at one stage but that amalgamation had taken place; Lacken was at one time divided into four quarters.

Patrick Holligan turns up as owning a quarry in Ballyknockan in Griffith's valuation of the early 1850s, but he is the only person who can be traced as having a definite connection with both Ballyknockan and Kilbride. Another family name which crops up in the two places is Doyle; but it is a common surname in Leinster and the families may not be connected. The Kilbride Doyles must have been well-known stonecutters and their headstone in Manor Kilbride graveyard bears the occupational insignia of a compass and square on one corner and what appears to be a church bell and ruler on the other. The Ballyknockan Doyles were accomplished self-taught sculptors.

Detail from the Doyle family headstone in Manor Kilbride graveyard showing stonemason's insignia

A second great wave of large-scale building got under way in Dublin in the 1820s as Catholics began to have the confidence and wherewithal to build large churches. This began in advance of Catholic Emancipation in 1829 and accelerated after it. With increased prosperity after the famine and a now resurgent Catholic Church throughout the country, the stonecutters' skills were in great demand. Three Dublin churches built in the pre-famine period used Ballyknockan stone extensively; these were St Francis Xavier's, Gardiner St (1829-32), St Andrew's, Westland Row, built between 1832 and 1837 and St Paul's, Arran Quay, which was begun in 1835, with portico, bell-turret and cupola added in 1843.

A fact alluded to by T.M. O'Reilly, a member of the O'Reilly

St. Francis Xavier's Church, Gardiner St., Dublin. It appears to have been the first large structure using Ballyknockan granite

Church of St. Andrew, Westland Row, Dublin. The first church to be built on a major thoroughfare in Dublin; the Ballyknockan stonecutters benefitted greatly from the resurgence of Catholic church building in the Dublin area

stonecutting family, who became a writer and journalist, suggests that the supply of stone used for the Jesuit Church in Gardiner St. could have been the first big job undertaken by Olligan. He states that the first wagon to enter Ballyknockan was known as the *St Xavier* and was a present from the fathers of the Gardiner St. Church to Patrick Olligan.

Tradition has it that the work done by Olligan and Duffy included the facade of the Catholic chapel in Valleymount, the stonecutters local place of worship. Records held in the parish show that the parish priest, Fr Finney, who died in 1833, had a tomb built for himself by Paul Duffy. It is now beneath the floor of the church. The Valleymount church was erected in 1803 to succeed a penal chapel at Annacarney.

In 1838 the Ordnance Survey fieldworkers go on to inform us that there were then two roads through Ballyknockan, 'both bad', and that the quarries provided wrought stone chiefly for Dublin, and all ornamental stone for miles around. The 160 labour force was divided into labourers who received 6 or 7 shillings a week, and smiths and stonecutters who received 15 to 20 shillings a week. There were then 30 landholders in the townland, all tenants at will paying a total annual rent of £163. Potatoes and oats were grown on the cultivated ground and the bottom ground provided blue marl for manure, the soil being rocky and light. Sheep grazed the hills.

In the decade between the census of 1841 and 1851 Ballyknockan became big enough to be designated a 'town', the population increasing from a total of 351 in 1841 to 430 in 1851, 353 living in the town and 77 in the rural portion. This represents an increase of 22.6% over the famine period – the stone trade was obviously booming. The number of houses increased in the same period from 53 to 68.

By 1852 three other quarries besides that of Olligan were in operation in Ballyknockan. Griffith's valuation contains the following details:

Bryan Hanlon – office, land and quarry (1 acre, 3 roods, 10 perches); total valuation 5s.

Patrick Reilly – Quarry (3 acres, 3 roods, 10 perches); total valuation 10s.

John Brady – House, offices, land and quarry 93 acres, 3 roods, 33 perches); total valuation £17, 15s. of which the quarry alone was valued at £15.

Patrick Holligan – offices, land and quarry (3 acres, 1 rood, 26 perches); total valuation £31, 10s – quarry alone £30.

The stonecutters' local place of worship in Valleymount. Originally built in 1803, the facade is later and displays to perfection the stonecutters' craft. It's exotic style is said to be modelled on churches which Ballyknockan men saw in Mexico while working there in the last century

It can be seen from this that Holligan had the most valuable quarry, followed by Brady and Reilly with a small concern owned by Hanlon. It is interesting that two of the surnames here, Reilly and Brady are associated with County Cavan; while the Reillys claim to have come from there, according to Brady family tradition they came to Ballyknockan from Golden Hill.

A study of subsequent valuation office records shows the changes of quarry ownership over the years. By 1862 James Freeman had taken over Hanlon's quarry; Patrick Reilly had taken over Holligan's and Peter Bryan had moved into Reilly's original one. Hanlon and Hollogan disappear as quarry-owners altogether. The disappearance of Holligan is noteworthy as his had been the largest quarry. The family tradition is that they gave up quarrying and turned to farming in their native Kilbride locality.

The Joy family sold its land in the area including Ballyknockan in 1864.

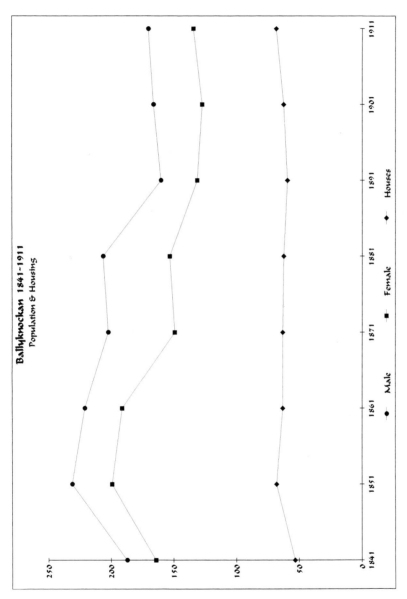

Nineteenth century population trends in Ballyknockan reflecting demand for granite. Growth is seen to over the famine decade and then a decline until the 1870s when there is an upswing. The 1880s show a decrease again with modest growth again up to 1911

In the advertisement for sale the following quarry-owners are listed together with their annual rent:

Patrick Reilly	£30
John Brady	£20 10s.
Patrick Reilly	£15 10s.
James Freeman	£10
Michael Doyle	£10
Peter Bryan	£10
Christopher McEvoy	£5
James Byrne	£5
Robert Osborne	£5
Michael Nowlan	£5

Three of these names, Freeman, Doyle, McEvoy and Osborne were to become well-known stonecutting families.

All of these tenants in 1864 held their land from year to year, determined on 1 August. The quarries were so close to each other that they were not properly mapped – the boundary between one and the next being known to the quarrymen but probably not to the landlord.

By 1874 Thomas M. O'Reilly had taken over his father Patrick's quarry and Robert Osborne's quarry was taken over by William Osborne. Thomas O'Reilly and William Osborne later became partners. The Osbornes trace their origins to Rathnabo and were probably quarrying and cutting field stones in that area before coming to Ballyknockan. A widespread and persistent legend states that they were quarrying a stone out of a field one day when they discovered a pot of gold under it. This set them up, and they obtained the quarry in Ballyknockan shortly afterwards. The gold was said to have been hidden by a highwayman Cock-a-Hoof, who eluded capture by the ruse of turning the shoes of his horse backwards. Cock-a-Hoof was said to have been born in Ballyknockan and a fine representation of him can be seen on the gable end of what was the Osborne house in Ballyknockan, now the Ballyknockan Inn. The McEvoys enter the scene when, according to Mary McEvoy of the Brook, her grandfather came to work for the Farringtons in Ballyknockan and eventually married a girl called Costello.

2

The working day

There were three categories of workers in the quarries – quarrymen, black-smiths and stonecutters.

'When my father was serving his time with Osborne', says Rosie O'Reilly, 'there were four apprentices there at the time – my father, my uncle Tommy, Bob Osborne and Mick Doyle. They were working a job for St. Audeon's, High Street. They worked from six o'clock in the morning to six in the evening and you got off at half eight in the morning for a cup of tea. They came home for their dinner in the middle of the day. In the dark evenings they used only work till five. They worked till half past twelve Saturdays. In latter years, when my father had his own quarries, they started at eight o'clock and finished at five. They were always paid on Saturdays.'

A quarryman, Johnny McDonnell, used to start work at eight o'clock and finish at five, although, if the work was there, they would work late in the summer. He remembers, winter mornings, going in and standing around as it was too dark to do any work; artificial light came later, gas at first. Rosie

An early photograph of workers in the quarries. Some are stonecutters as their white aprons can be seen around their waists

A group of workers in O'Reilly's qaurry in Ballinastockan: they are, from the left, Jack Byrne, Paddy Lawlor, Paddy Byrne, Tommy O'Reilly and Peter O'Reilly, for many years a Wicklow County Councillor, representing the Ballyknockan area

remembers a big job being done for Guinness, a gateway, she says. A night shift was got up to finish it, working by the light of gas lamps brought out from St. James' Gate: 'one set of men in bed, while another set was working,' as she puts it.

It was the job of the quarrymen to cut from the rock face blocks from which the skilled stonecutters would carve the finished product. They usually worked in twos. A line was made on the rock with a string and this line was cut in the rock with special quarry picks. Wedges were then placed at intervals along this line and driven in by the quarrymen with sledges, one following the other. As the wedges sunk into the granite they were replaced by bigger and bigger ones. They were never allowed touch the bottom of the hole in which they were inserted as the vibration would come back to the sledge; the pressure required was outwards not downwards. Other pairs of quarrymen would be working at another section of the quarry face, perhaps four or five pairs in all. These could serve up to 100 stonecutters.

Sometimes there would be scores of wedges on the same line. Jim Mahon of Carrigacurra remembers his father telling him that at one time they used to use wooden wedges. In the evening before they left they used to pour water on them, and sometimes the expansion of the wood would split the stone for them overnight. The block of granite was then moved by crane onto bogies on tracks and pulled by horse up to the sheds were the stonecutters were working at their benches.

Granite has a grain in it like wood. As much as possible the rock was split along the freeway, which was the same as cutting timber with the grain. The direction against it was the crossway. In Ballyknockan the granite is aligned so that the freeway runs east west or as the quarrymen put it 'with the rising sun'.

Sometimes the rock was dislodged by blasting, especially in tight corners. A hole for holding the powder for blasting was made in this way. A bar with a four way split on one end called a jumper was placed on the rock and held by one man as another struck it with a sledge; each time the jumper was hit it was turned. As the hole got deeper, bigger and bigger jumpers were used until one about 12 feet high was needed, struck by a 56 pound sledge. As Dónal McEvoy explains it was only necessary to lift the sledge once as after the first blow it would bounce back up, but the man on the sledge would still grunt with each strike. The hole was kept wet by pouring water into it and straw was put on top of it to prevent water splashing into the workers' faces with each blow.

When the hole was deep enough the powder was poured into it. It was tamped down with a round-faced bar. Dónal often did this as a boy without thinking. When he reflects on it now he sees how dangerous it was – one spark from the bar and the whole lot would have gone up. Paper was then stuffed in and a fuse which was lit from a safe distance.

Stonecutting tools

3

Stonecutters

In the early years of this century an apprentice stonecutter worked for free in his first month; he then got 12 shillings per week for a year. Each year after that he would get an extra 10 shillings until he reached a wage of £3.5.0 and the status of a journeyman. At the same time the quarrymen were receiving £2.15.0.

Ballyknockan stonecutters' craftmanship embellishes many part of West Wicklow. This is an old forge entrance in Hollywood. Another example can be seen in the main street in Blessington

Surviving wagebooks for one quarry for 1918 show that while most men were working six days a week they were on short time and were taking home on average about £2 per week. The number of hours worked varied very much from week to week.

The stonecutters were the elite of the quarry with their corduroy trousers, white aprons, and in the early days, clogs – later heel and toe capped boots. The people of Ballyknockan were always very musical and it was said that "the gaffer" Brady liked them to hum a quick tune while working as the

Burgage graveyard, Blessington, has many examples of unusual headstones in granite; some have been identified as being by the Doyle family of Ballyknockan

Fine detail from the Bank of Ireland (National Branch), College Green, Dublin

mallets would work faster. The whole village was alive to the "chip chip" of the stonecutters. Their characteristic instruments were the wooden mallet and chisel. They also used squares and punches.

Johnny McDonnell remembers the stonecutters striking because a young man from the Tóchar was taken on to serve his time as a stonecutter: 'he was only a chap going to serve his time as a stonecutter, but because his father wasn't a stonecutter, he wasn't allowed in'. Johnny's father was a farmer; this did not matter because the work of a quarryman was not regarded as a trade. Stonecutters would carve their own mallets at home. The usual timber from which they were made was boxwood. The finished mallet would be placed up the chimney to season.

4

Blacksmiths

Joe Toomey, from Carrigacurra, started 'nippering' as he called it, in the forge in Ballyknockan in 1929. When the picks got blunt or 'stiff' as the men termed it, they would knock them off the handle and replace them with sharp ones. Joe's job was to gather these up, blow the fire, wheel the picks in, sharpen them, and bring them out again to the men. Mary McEvoy's grandfather also started in the forge 'as a nipper', she says.

As well as sharpening the tools, the smiths also made them in the quarries. This was done from steel which came from Hadfield in England. In 1929 there were 95 men employed in Osborne and Brady's quarry and these were scattered around in sheds engaged in cutting the stone, 15 or 16 men in each. There were around 300 picks and wedges in the quarry, all the property of Osborne and Brady, but the mens' tools were their own, highly prized, and locked in their own box in the quarry overnight.

Anvil in forge

5

Industrial unrest

There was much unrest in the quarries in Ballyknockan in the 1890s. A protracted strike ended in 1891 on the intervention of no less a person than the Archbishop of Dublin, William Walsh. He had visited the Parish of Valleymount and met Mr Brady, the quarry owner and Mr White, the representative of the men. Archbishop Walsh addressed an open letter, which was printed as a pamphlet, to the quarry-owners and the workers congratulating them on the settlement of their dispute and putting forward his proposals for the setting up of a Dublin Conciliation Council on the lines of the London body, and so Ballyknockan gained for itself a footnote in the annals of Irish labour history.

There were more problems at the end of the decade and a Mr Clancy, secretary of the Stonecutters Union of Ireland, which had been established in Cork, visited Ballyknockan in September 1898 and was well received by the men. He informed them that 'in those districts where we are organised as a union we have struck a standard rate of 30 shillings for a 57 hour week, having all our members stop work at 2.00 p.m. on Saturday, whereas previous to joining our union, the majority of those men worked 63 hours per week and until 6.00 p.m. on Saturdays for 24 shillings per week.' Delegates from Cork began to visit Ballyknockan often in the following years and some time later another strike in the quarries was averted after a friendly meeting between the quarry-owners and the local representative of the union, John Doyle.

A local quarry worker named Toomey was a union organiser in the early year of this century and Mary McEvoy remembers a few lines of a song about him. His nickname was *Sap*.

> Come all ye boys stand together
> Stand up for the *Sap* every man
> He's the next thing to Jim Larkin
> The pride of the hardworking man.

Nicholas Ryan in his study of quarrying in Co. Dublin, *The Sparkling Granite*, speaks of much solidarity between quarries, including Ballyknockan, in times of industrial unrest, although on one occasion the Ballyknockan 'gaffers' settled first and so cornered much of the work.

Ryan gives a very impressive litany of nicknames from his area and, of course, they were very common also in a closeknit community like Ballyknockan. A little story Dónal McEvoy tells shows how a nickname could originate. A young man started work in the quarry and was asked to get the poker from the forge one day to light a fire. He did not run fast enough and from that day was called *Coldpoker*.

Many of the quarry workers at the turn of the century were attached to the organisation known at the Irish National Foresters. This acted largely as a mutual benefit society and Ballyknockan had its own branch (no. 1004). In 1913 Peter O'Reilly was its chief ranger in Ballyknockan.

6

Transport

In a survey of Irish granites published in 1889, it was stated that the principal granite used for cut stone purposes in the Dublin area was from Ballyknockan, Stepaside and Glencullen. The Ballyknockan stone cost about 4 shillings per cubic foot in the rough, and carriage, all by road, was about 5 shillings per ton (there was 11 cubic feet to the ton). The fact that the Ballyknockan granite could be expertly dressed at the quarry cut down on the cost as regards the cost of labour at the building site and the tonnage which would have to be quarried.

George Wilkinson, writing in his *Practical Geology and Ancient Architecture of Ireland* (Dublin & London, 1845), gives a good example of this. He states that the station and offices then lately erected on the Dublin and Kingstown (now Dún Laoghaire) railway were built of Blessington (more than likely from Ballyknockan) stone. He points out that it was more economical to bring the stone all the way from Blessington, a distance of about 20 miles than use local granite.

The cost of working the stone into sills, steps, quoins etc. was one shilling and six pence per lineal foot. Moulds' chamfering, cornices, string courses and columns were dearer again, Ballyknockan being about one shilling and three pence dearer than Stepaside. The Ballyknockan was regarded as being better stone, both in colour and quality. Its white-grey colour was distinctive, but when weathered took on much the same colour as other granites. In Séamus Murphy's fine book *Stone Mad*, and old stonecutter or 'stoney' raves about it, calling it 'the oatmeal'. It was also more easily worked. In 1889 it was possible to import Aberdeen granite, but its price was about double that of Ballyknockan.

Special long carts were employed to transport the granite to Dublin and other places. The carters are spoken of with great respect in Ballyknockan today, their job often entailing great hardship. They would leave Ballyknockan in the early evening and wend their way to the Dublin building sites in time for their cargo to be unloaded first thing the next morning. The way out of Ballyknockan was over the bog road, now submerged beneath the waters of the Poulaphuca reservoir.

The night journey was undertaken maybe three times a week in hail, rain and even snow. Johnny McDonnell remembers seeing nine or ten drays going along the bog road. Each horse could haul 30 cwt of stone and for bigger loads

*Norton's of the Embankment, where many of the Ballyknockan draymen stopped for
a drink on their nocturnal journey to Dublin with their cargo of granite*

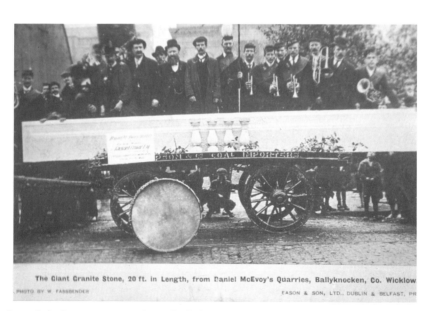

The Giant Granite Stone, 20 ft. in Length, from Daniel McEvoy's Quarries, Ballyknocken, Co. Wicklow

*One of the largest pieces to leave Ballyknockan. It was for Glencairn, the home of
'Boss' Croker in south County Dublin. It was made in Daniel McEvoy's quarry and
paraded through the streets of Dublin headed by the Ballyknockan Stonecutters'
Band in a display of Irish industries at the turn of the century*

four wheeled wagons were used, pulled by four horses. Farmers would often take up haulage to supplement their income; in Pat Foster's early days (Pat, of Ballyknockan, worked all his life in the quarries) they earned 2s. 6d. for the journey in and out. At a place called Norton's of the Embankment, variously called a 'shebeen', 'dosshouse' and 'hole in the wall', they would stop and have a few drinks, and even sleep for a while. They would then set out again and reach the building site at seven or eight in the morning as work commenced.

Stopping for a few drinks on the way home they would often fall asleep before they had even reached Terenure and the horses would walk all the way home to Ballyknockan unguided. The dogs of Ballyknockan would recognise the jingle of the cart of its master and run out to greet him. Johnny McDonnell observes however that if a drayman fell asleep with a heavy load on the way in, the horse would stop in the middle of the road until the driver woke up and started it off again.

Accidents did occur. In June 1897 a man from Burgage, who had been getting a lift home from a stonecutter fell off in a weakness and two stone carts following ran over him killing him. There is also a curious stone cross with a cross crudely inscribed on it near the Valleymount end of what was the bog road and it is said to mark the spot where a cartman met with an accident, whether he was killed or not is disputed.

One of the biggest stones to leave Ballyknockan was for Glencairn, the house owned by 'Boss' Croker. It formed part of the great parade of Irish industries which took place in Dublin at the turn of the century and was paraded through the streets accompanied by the Ballyknockan band. The extra-large dray for this stone was made by Andy Cavanagh, a carpenter from Baile Mhór. Carpenters were continually employed in making and repairing the wheels for the drays.

A large number of horses were needed of course for such a transport undertaking and the Osborne's had a row of stables and a stable yard. They grew their own oats and barley in land near Ballymore Eustace and it was stored in a big barn in Ballyknockan.

In 1896 it was proposed to extend the Dublin to Blessington and Poulaphouca steam tram through Valleymount to Ballyknockan and on over the Wicklow gap, so that it could be used to transport stone from the quarries to Dublin. The scheme was over-ambitious for what was already not a too successful line and there was a lot of local opposition and the plan was dropped. William Osborne brought the first lorry for the transport of stone into the quarries. Rosie O'Reilly remembers that it was a Thornycroft.

7

Education

For many years the education of the children of the Ballyknockan quarry workers was catered for in the small building, still standing, called 'Master Black's'. This pay-school was one of a number of 'hedge-schools' in the parish going back to the beginning of the 19th century and probably further. In 1866 an attempt was made to have the Ballyknockan taken up by the board of education. On 2 April of that year a teacher called John Wexted commenced a school in the building. He had taken over from a previous teacher who was convicted in the assizes court for gross misconduct, the nature of which we are not told.

Wexted in his application states that he had taught for the previous 15 years in Ballymore Eustace. He had been recommended to the people of Ballyknockan by the board's inspector, who described him as having no training in a model school but was of respectable acquirements, excellent character and a painstaking and skillful teacher. He had no other occupation and lived in his own room in the school.

The inspector, pressing Ballyknockan's case for a school, stated that the two nearest schools were that at Blackditches (Valleymount) one mile distant which had an average attendance of 78 pupils and 'Lacken chapel school' two miles distant, conducted by a hedge school master of humble acquirements.

The inspector felt that a school was badly needed in Ballyknockan as there were a great number of men working in the quarries and they wished their children to be educated according to the course laid down by the board. On the day that he visited the school it had an attendance of 23 males and seven females, the average attending for the previous six months being about 23. He felt that this might improve as the school had been started at the worst time of the year, and that up to 70 would attend. The pupils paid one pence, one and a half pence, tow pence or three pence per week, probably depending on the level they were at, this gave the teacher an annual income of about six pounds.

The schoolhouse was described as being of granite and mortar, slated and dashed externally and whitewashed internally. It had been built on a site given by the landlord and was rent-free forever. It was in a fair state of repair and two lattice windows and two ordinary windows. There was one schoolroom furnished with four new desks, but no blackboard, clock or suitable desk for the teacher.

School was held six days a week and religious instruction would be taught for a half an hour a day and for two hours on Saturdays. The school would be under the management of the Rev. John O'Reilly of Valleymount but would be open to all denominations.

The inspector pointed out to the board that there was no other recognised national school in the area in the populous parish of Boystown having a male teacher, but despite this the application was turned down on the grounds that the average attendance was not high enough.

The last teacher in the school was Gerard Black, 'Master Black'. Father Browne describes him at the turn of the century:

> At the outskirts of Ballyknockan stood an old disused school-house that had been built by the marquis of Waterford for the children of his tenants. The last teacher was a Master Black. When the National School was set up at Monavalla (Valleymount) a considerable number of the children still stayed with Master Black even though he charged for instruction; one penny a week for the first book, twopence a week for the second, and threepence a week would put a scholar through the rest of the course. Martin presumed that the teacher must have been very proficient if he could maintain his school in spite of the fact that education was free in the National School.

> 'The chief attraction,' said Joe, 'was that Master Black played the bagpipes during school hours. He had a big long whisker and was fond of a sup. He used to run dances on the quiet until the priest got after him. After his retirement he went to live in Dublin, but he often came back for a holiday, going round among all his past pupils.'

8

Social life

Music played a big part in the lives of the quarry workers. Going as far back as the 1880s they had their own brass and reed band. Their new band house was opened with a gala concert in the village in July 1888, and the programme included 'several fine operatic and popular airs'. Brass bands were very popular at the time, particularly among work forces. A brass band festival was arranged to take place in Poulaphuca one Sunday in early September 1898. Two bands from Dublin, the St Kevin's, Protestant Row Band and the Dublin Bricklayers' Band and the Ballyknockan Cross Pikes Band were due to take part. The Blessington Steam Tram Company laid on special trips from the city and conveyed in all 500 bandsmen and their supporters from Dublin.

The Ballyknockan Brass and Reed Band. A stonecutters' band existed from the 1880s but divided into two rival factions, the Parnellites and the 'Whigs' at the time of the Parnell split. The picture was taken in 1928 and includes Joe Brady, Kit McEvoy, Paddy O'Reilly, Rock Osborne, Barny Quinn, Peter Keogh, Tom Cahill, George Flynn, Christy Keogh, Billy McEvoy, Jim Cullen, Billy Brady, Eddie McDonnell, Odie McEvoy, Tom Osborne, Bob Keogh, Bill Keogh, Patsy Keogh, Christy Brady, Jimmy Cahill, Jack McEvoy, Jerry Behan, Dan Cullen, Anthony Lambert, Tommy O'Reilly, Jimmy Flynn, Jim Doyle, John Nolan and Larry Byrne

A general view of the main quarry

Due to an oversight, the Ballyknockan men were unable to take part as they had forgotten the Kilcullen sports, at which they were engaged to play, were on that day.

A series of rows broke out, due, it was reported, to a Carrigacurra man (Carrigacurra is the a neighbouring townland to Ballyknockan) engaging in an altercation with the major of the Protestant Row band. The row reached such proportions that the police from Hollywood were not able to cope with it. Peace was restored when one of the Dublin bands played some airs dear to the Wicklowmen's hearts. It was agreed, at the end of the day, that an enjoyable time was had by all, despite the general fracas earlier on.

Wrestling, particularly on Sunday afternoons, was a favourite sport. In the book *In Monavalla*, the curate in 'Monavalla', Valleymount, goes walking on the bog road to Ballyknockan:

> He stepped to the grass margin to keep well clear of a horse and trap that he heard coming at a fast pace from the direction of Monavalla. When the horse drew level it was brought to a sudden halt by the driver who lifted his hat in salutation.

> 'I was on my way to your house, Father, to pay my respects; but Jack Rooney told me that you were going over to see the quarries. Sit up an I'll take you there.'

> Martin sat opposite the driver, a thin spare man with a bristling grey moustache and a black bowler hat which he wore tilted over his poll.

'I'm Joe Dermody', the man said in a pleasant voice. 'I was at the post-office to telephone about a consignment of stone for a new bank in Carlow.'

As they drove on Dermody pointed out places of local historical significance to the curate. He indicated with the handle of his whip a green patch on the verge of the bog, directly under a gently-sloping bank:

'That's where the wrestling matches used to be held long ago on a Sunday afternoon. The spectators watched from the bank.'

Martin expressed surprise that such a sodden plot of ground should be chosen for an arena.

''Twas a nice, soft spot for a fall,' Joe said with a smile. The last of the contests was held when I was a chap. I saw the famous "Brasheen" Cullen, a stone-cutter, throw 'Baldy' Delaney of the Queen's County.'

Martin learned that considerable stakes were laid on the outcome. No special costumes were worn, the wrestlers just took off their coats and waist-coats and set at one another in a 'catch-as-catch-can'. The issue was decided on the best of three falls.

The quarry workers worked hard and some of them drank hard. Writing in 1862, a Fr O' Rorke of the parish, in a letter to the archbishop, stated that 'granite quarries are extensively worked in our parish – these quarries open out a depot for all immoral, corrupt, and ready-made vagabonds'. He did not think much of one of the quarry-owners either, comparing him to Victor Emmanuel, who was in dispute with the Pope at the time. His jaundiced view of the quarries may perhaps be explained by the fact that he had been at law with the Ballyknockan Victor Emmanuel over land and lost.

Like every other village and parish in Ireland Gaelic games were taken up with enthusiasm at the end of the last century. The Ballyknockan '98s were formed in 1887. Under the tutelage of T.M. O'Reilly and William Osborne they remained for many years prominent in county competitions. Like many another team of the day their exploits were celebrated by local poets:

They came from Ballyknockan
With their bands and banners green
To lower the pride of Baltinglass
Upon Athreany's field.

In latter years the old Osborne barn was used for dances and showing films.

The 'Barn Cinema'

9

Community unrest

The most famous incident in the history of Ballyknockan concerns the eviction of two elderly ladies from their house in the 1880s. Some years previous to this trouble had been brewing between the tenants in Ballyknockan and the landlord, Lord Waterford. The landlord's main antagonist was T.M. O'Reilly, a strong Parnellite. T.M. was educated at Blackrock College and became a journalist with the *Kildare Observer* and later with the *Leinster Leader*. All property owners were tenants at will and various tenant organisations and the parish priest tried to get Waterford to agree to short leases but in replies from his London club, he refused. In one confrontation, it was said, an eviction was attempted on Christmas Eve, but was thwarted by the people.

For many years two men named Lawlor and Norton carried on a small trade by quarrying surface stone on the mountainside, thereby giving employment to local farmers. In November 1884 Waterford served writs on them to prevent them quarrying any more stone on their holdings and claiming dam-

The plaque on the house twice rebuilt by the Ballyknockan community overnight: it states: 'The emergency land-grabber defeated here 1888 – God save Ireland'

ages for those already quarried. A year later the landlord made determined efforts against O'Reilly by taking legal proceedings against him. When this failed the victory was celebrated in the area by bonfires on the hills.

One version of the eviction story has it that the house was given by the landlord to a schoolteacher who had set up school in Ballyknockan and that on the death of the schoolteacher it had passed on to two nieces. The landlord then tried to get back possession in favour of another man, but this man was prevented from doing so by Bridget Mulvey, one of the nieces. The would-be owner then bought possession of the holding from Thomas Panton, a large landowner in the area. On gaining ownership he then, in the dead of night, demolished the cottage. Local people were incensed by this however and came to Bridget Mulvey's assistance and the house was rebuilt on a Saturday night between midnight and morning, to the astonishment of local people travelling the bog road to Mass on Sunday morning.

The 'grabber' was not to be outdone however and he came, and with the help of his sons, pulled the house down again and the poor woman inside barely escaped with her life. Bridget Mulvey then went to court and won her action against her adversary. He was officially evicted from the holding on 16 January 1888. Once again the local people rallied to the old lady's assistance and rebuilt her house for her. Here is how the event was described in the *Leinster Leader* of 11 February 1888, almost certainly written by T.M. O'Reilly:

> Monday (6 February) witnessed a demonstration that will long be re-membered in Ballyknockan and the surrounding district of West Wicklow and North Kildare. The occasion of the proceedings was the reinstate-ment in her little holding and the building of a home for a poor desolate creature whose house was leveled by the rapacious grabber of her plot of land. The facts of her case, the grabbing of her humble property by a man of her own locality are so recent and so well known as to render recapitulation unnecessary.
>
> The night had shrouded the majestic proportions of the neighbour-ing mountains in glittering snow, as morning dawned the hardy mountaineers saw they should have to trudge over snowy paths, though moor and glen, to reach the scene of operation. But neither the forbid-ding frowns of Wicklow's twin monarchs Old Lug or Mullaclevaun, nor the chilling northern breeze that swept the hillsides and the plain could cool the ardour of the enthusiastic thousands who thronged from the glens and dales and craggy hillsides of Boystown, Lacken, Hollywood, Dunlavin, Ballymore, and even Ballinacarey [*sic*] County Dublin, to prove this practical sympathy for the oppressed and their detestation of the grabber.
>
> At quite an early hour, work was already in full swing. The masons, carpenters and numerous others engaged in drawing the material, pre-

paring the stone and mortar etc., performed their unselfish tasks with a heartiness and vigour that no hope of self or greed of gold could call forth. Heedless of toil, undisturbed by the numerous witticisms and jokes of the funny folks around, cheered by the loud and oft-repeated applause of the vast crowds that witnessed the proceedings, the regular craftsmen and amateur workers, without flag or pause, prosecuted the operations till the shades of evening fell upon a comfortable all but complete.

With the evening came the most remarkable and soul-stirring part of the day's proceeding. The poor woman for whom the house was built did not appear during the day, and now steps were taken to conduct her in processional order to her new home.

Working abroad

Sir Edwin Lutyens came to the McEvoy's of Granite House in 1935 to look into the possibility of using Ballyknockan granite in the building of Liverpool Cathedral. He had already used it in the building of his fine War Memorial at Islandbridge. Due to the high shipping costs, however, it could not be used, the stone eventually coming from Cornwall. But there was an export from Ballyknockan – people; many Ballyknockan men spent years working on Liverpool Cathedral.

Jimmy McDonnell went to work in Barnacullia and in Wolverhampton where there were both Barnacullia and Ballyknockan men. They went to work in Scotland as well. Ballyknockan men used walk over the hills to Glencullen on a Sunday and return the following Saturday afternoon. They had a race one time, between a cyclist doing the journey by road and walker over the hills; the walkers won.

Mary McEvoy of the Brook remembers her relations going to England carrying their tools on their backs. They went to places like Ebbw Vale and Bristol. Peter was working on the Liverpool Docks. He fell into the sea and was dragged down as he had his tools strapped around his waist. He managed to undo them and so saved himself. Tools were usually handed down from father to son and they were a big loss to Peter. Many tools still remain in Ballyknockan.

More Dublin work

In 1964, 71 year old Jimmy Freeman, a stonecutter for 60 years and the fourth generation of his family at the trade. Jim recalled rebuilding O'Connell Street after the 1916 Rising: 'the carved stonework for numbers 5, 6, 7, 14, 15, 28, 29 and 31 came

The Fusiliers' Arch, St. Stephen's Green, Dublin, worked on by the Freeman family of stonecutters

Entrance to Power's Distillery, Thomas St., Dublin, now the National College of Art and Design. Michael Freeman remembers as a child been shown the beautiful granite scrolls by his father and told with pride how they were worked by members of his family

from the Freeman quarry'. He recalled working on the Fusiliers' Arch entrance to St. Stephen's Green, and on the stonework for Glasnevin Schools and Wesley College. Michael Freeman remembers his uncle telling him as a boy how he did one side of the door surround on the Distillery building in Thomas Street (now the College of Art and Design).

When Johnny McDonnell went to work for Osborne and Brady around

1940 there were about 120 men working in the quarry. They had a huge contract which they had been working on for some years restoring the Four Courts in Dublin after it had been damaged at the outbreak of the Civil War. They were cutting ashlar blocks and had got saws to do the job. There were three blades working abreast, day and night sometimes. Johnny remembers cutting the die stone for a 14' high Celtic Cross which was interlaced in Ballyknockan by an artist called Robert Preston as a memorial to Fr John Murphy in Wexford.

Mary McEvoy remembers her three brothers working on blocks for the docks in Galway in 1938. They worked so hard that she reckoned that it contributed to their deaths. The stone was transported by a local man, Hamilton, all the way to the west. 'I hear that the stones were washed away since' she says sadly.

By this time all the great building were no longer being built of granite and the quarries relied more and more on grave monuments and small decorative pieces for buildings. An example of the latter was the work done by Peter P. O'Reilly for houses on the Navan Road, Dublin in 1934. Each house was supplied with six granite window sills, six centres for bay windows, 12 knees for bay windows and caps for doorways. The total cost was £4.17.6 per house.

An examination of the 1901 census reveals that there were 61 families in Ballyknockan. Occupational structure of the heads of household breaks down as follows:

Stonecutter or stonemason	27
Labourer	2
Drayman	1
Farm Labourer	4
Shoemaker (Thomas Pender)	1
Author and Journalist (Thomas O'Reilly)	1
Cutstone Contractor)	1
Farmer	9
Blacksmith	2
Quarry Owner	1
Quarryman	2
Master Stonecutter (Joseph Brady)	1

12

Michael Collins

Dónal McEvoy tells us that Christopher McEvoy was the first of that surname to quarry stone in Ballyknockan. He took over a quarry from Farringtons
– they were a brother and sister, and Christopher married the sister. The first
job that Dónal's father worked on was on the spire of the Presbyterian Church
in Parnell Square, known to Dubliners as Findlater's Church. The architect
brought Dónal's father up on the spire to see it and he was afraid of his life.
Some of the jobs which the McEvoys worked on were the labour Exchange in
Lord Edward Street, opposite Dublin Castle, Eason's, O'Connell Street, and
a bank in Naas.

Two particular jobs were a water tower in the Curragh Camp and a
church in Carlow town. The Curragh job was done around 1928 and necessi-
tated making the joints in the stone water-tight. They made them of tongue
and groove, which would be quite unusual in stone. Thirty foot granite columns were ordered for the church. The building was to have no downpipes
and so holes were bored down through the granite. These had to be done by
hand as they were afraid of going too close to the edge of the column and so
splitting the rock.

R.D.S. entrance, Dublin. Built with granite from McEvoy's quarry

Unveiling of memorial in Wicklow granite at the birthplace of Michael Collins,
Sam's Cross, Co. Cork, Easter 1965

Building a new facade for the R.D.S. in Dublin was a particularly big undertaking for the McEvoys. Collen Brothers were the builders and the tender was worth £35,000. There was a clause attached however. A penalty would be incurred if any section of the work started was not completed between the holding of the Spring Show, the Horse Show and the Bull Show. Dónal's father gathered the men together in the quarry and explained the situation to them. To a man they agreed to the contract – there would be work in it for them for at least three years. They started at six each morning, the women bringing them breakfast at half past eight. After breaks for dinner and tea they worked by the light of lamps in the quarry till midnight.

Dónal remembers one night a strange car pulling into Brady's yard. It had come all the way from Cork and carried representatives from a committee set up to erect a memorial to Michael Collins at his birthplace, Sam's Cross. The men from Cork could not believe it when they saw a picture of Collins on the wall in Brady's house when they walked in. Brady's were great admirers of Collins and so is Dónal and he could not but join in the scheme. The committee was looking for a piece of Wicklow granite to mark the 'Big Fella's' birthplace and had been directed to Ballyknockan.

The Ballyknockan people were curious as to why a more local stone was not selected as being much more convenient for the job. They were told a moving story as to why only Wicklow granite would be acceptable. When the Cork committee thought about erecting such a memorial they approached the sisters of Collins, then still alive, and asked them for their opinion on a

Government Bulidings, Merrion St. Upper, Dublin. Opened in 1911 as the Royal College of Science the basement level contains Ballknockan granite

suitable monument. They immediately replied that they would like Wicklow granite. When asked why, they went on to tell the story of Mick's last visit to his home place.

When he came home all the local people gathered into the house for a party with singing and dancing, which went on till the early hours. As people began to drift home a local man piped up and asked Mick a question; 'you have been all over Ireland, Mick; and met people from every county, which of them do you like the best?' Mick's answer was, without any hesitation 'the people from County Wicklow.' the next day, according to Dónal, he was killed at Béal na mBláth. That is why Michael's sisters wanted Wicklow granite for the memorial.

It was decided that a natural field stone, rather than a cut quarried stone would be the most suitable for the memorial. A search for a suitable boulder was undertaken and one was found above the old mines at Hero near Glendalough. It was a good distance from the road. A garage man who came out from Spawell could not budge it. Then a digger with caterpillar wheels was brought in and took three days to get it to the road. It weighed about 110 tons. When eventually it was got moving a digger had to go before it all the way down to Glendalough for fear that it would run away. It was like a circus all the way to Cork, avoiding small bridges for fear that they would collapse under the weight.

*A group of stonecutters, mainly from Ballyknockan, working on the restoration of
the Four Courts, Dublin in the 1920s. It includes Christy Keogh, John Cullen, Tom
and Pat Osborne, Paddy Toomey, Pat Costello, Bob Cahill, Jim Doyle, Dinny
Cullen, Neddy Cullen, Mick Osborne, Jack White, John Flynn, Paddy Cullen,
Paddy Flynn, Jack Cullen, Patsy Keogh, Kit McEvoy, Paddy McEvoy, Peter
Keogh and Micky Kearns*

Most of the travelling was done at night with a Garda escort. It took
them 12 nights to reach Sam's Cross. A crane from Cork docks was positioned to lift the stone into place but when it tried to lift it it crashed down
with bits flying everywhere, scattering the crowd which had come to watch.
Finally it was lifted into place by a crane brought out from Killarney, which
was the width of the road. There was a great shout of joy when it was
eventually put in place. The Ballyknockan men who had travelled with it cut
a circular inset for a medallion. It was unveiled at Easter 1965.

13

The later years

Most of the stone from Ballyknockan in the 20th century came from the Osborne and Brady quarry. The two families sealed links which had been already forged through marriage by a business amalgamation. After the second world war it was widely believed that the granite was finished as far as the building trade was concerned with the introduction of re-inforced concrete. This turned out to be the case and shortly after the death of John Brady in the late 1950s the large quarry closed down for some years. However with the introduction of technology to slice the granite into slabs for cladding, the quarry was re-opened by the Creedon group in the mid-1960s. Building cladded by Ballyknockan granite include the Central Bank and the Civic Offices, both in Dublin.

The production of this cladding continues today, with a number of hand stonecutters continuing to produce high quality monumental and decorative work. Very few young people are involved in the work however and if the great tradition of craft work is to be carried on a training programme needs to be put in place urgently.

At work on Liverpool Cathedral around 1957. Included are Steve Hanna (Dublin), and the Ballyknockan men, Aby Osborne, Christy Keogh and Tom Cullen

Ned Mahon of Carrigacurra at work in
Creedon's quarry

Diamond-tipped machinery which now
cuts slices of granite for cladding

Civic Offices, Dublin cladded with Ballyknockan granite

The handcraft passed on to a younger generation; John McEvoy carving a name plaque

THE VILLAGE

14

The Village

GENERAL

Ballyknockan is not a village in the same way as Valleymount or Lacken, as some essential facilities are absent. There is a shop and petrol pumps, two public houses, a dispensary but no church or post office. The house beside the bridge over the Oghill Brook was formerly a school. One of the largest buildings housed a dancehall and cinema on the first floor and a cow byre on the ground floor. It is remembered as "the barn cinema". Recent decades have seen a great number of new houses on the approaches to and within the village itself. A considered approach to the design and location of new buildings is the greatest challenge facing the village today.

The view of Ballyknockan across the reservoir from Lacken or Valleymount is appropriately dominated by the huge crane and spoil heaps of Creedon's working quarry. The village seems to spill down the western flank of Moanbane. The houses and outbuildings are in fact built on five distinct terraces. Most of the houses are oriented north-west as a result. Only two houses face in a southerly direction – the Land League house (rebuilt 1888) and one county council cottage (built *c.*1900). The later cottages, built to house some of the families displaced by the reservoir, respect the established orientation by facing north-west.

THE ROAD NETWORK

All of the roads were present in some form in 1838. The most remarkable change is the loss to the reservoir of the original main road (the Bog Road) to Valleymount in favour of the more circuitous road from the south (1.5 km longer). Rough cobbling which provided grip for the drays transporting the cut granite can still be seen at the west, reservoir end of the present Bog Road. The road to Lacken was realigned northwards after 1838 and today the Old Road is disused for half of its length. The narrow road to the quarries has always been of considerable economic importance. The Sand, a road swinging west at the southern entry to the village and rejoining it at the north end is essentially the spine of the older part of the village, though it is too narrow for cars. Two narrower paths, the Pump and the Black Lane, connect the Sand with the present main road. The disused Horse Lane connected the centre of

43

Main road to Valleymount

The Horse Lane

the village with the Bog Road. The Bull Lane connected the Old Road with the quarry area on the Lacken side of the village. The Horse Lane, Bull Lane and Long Land Lane (running north from the main road) resemble the 'hollow ways' of abandoned medieval villages, as they are sunken well below the level of the land on each side of them. The Horse Lane is lined on its east side by an enormous field wall up to 2.55m (8'6") high and 1.85m (6') thick. A field path, now partly encroached upon by new houses, connected the Main Road, Old Road, Bull Lane and the quarry area. A number of other lanes and paths, mainly disused, lead to old quarry workings or former farmyards. The Stable Yard is a cul-de-sac of two-storey terraced houses and is the village's only street in the normal sense.

Field Path

Bridges

There are two bridges in the Ballyknockan area. The more northerly takes the road to Lacken over the Oghill/Troman Brook. It is pre-1838 in date. It is 3m (10') long and 5m (16') wide and has three 'eyes', spanned by flat stone lintels, giving it the appearance of a clapper bridge. It has slight, later cutwaters, i.e. pointed stonework on the upstream side designed to break the force of the water striking the bridge. The more southerly bridge may have replaced a fording point in more recent times. It has two eyes formed by large concrete culvert pipes and has concrete cutwaters.

Bridge over Oghill Brook

15

The Buildings

THEIR AGE

The earliest reliable maps of the district are those produced by the sappers of the Ordnance Survey in 1838 and engraved in 1839. They show that relatively few (35%) of the stone buildings which survive at Ballyknockan were built prior to that date. Some of these only survive as fragments of the original structures. The rest of the early buildings have disappeared. Some were probably dismantled for use in other buildings or field walls and a number in the area of the present quarry disappeared as the quarry expanded between 1838 and 1908. Twenty-four houses (40%) were erected throughout the village during this same period, presumably to house workers and activities associated with the growing prosperity of the settlement. The remaining 13 pre-bungalow houses (20%) were erected between 1908 and the present day. Ten of these are labourers' cottages built by the County Council between 1908 and about 1940. Half of these cottages housed people displaced by the flooding of the valley. They are similar to houses being built in many parts of Ireland at the time and are somewhat larger than those built around the turn of the last century. They are built of concrete whereas the earlier ones are of stone. As such, they mark the beginning of the move away from the local building material.

Figure 1: Age of buildings, etc. in Ballyknockan 1997

	Pre-1838	1838-1908	Post-1908
Houses	22	30	14
Outbuildings	14	45	18
Other buildings	1	7	7
Farmyards	7	5	3
Quarries	3	6	Nil

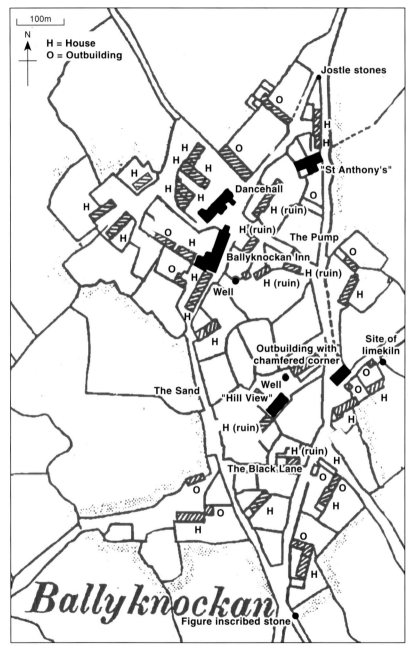

100m

N

H = House
O = Outbuilding

Jostle stones

O

H

H

"St Anthony's"

H

H

H

Dancehall

O

H

H (ruin)

H (ruin)

H (ruin)

The Pump

O

Ballyknockan Inn

O

O

H

H (ruin)

H

Well

H (ruin)

H

H

Outbuilding with
chamfered corner

Site of
limekiln

O

O

Well

O

H

The Sand

"Hill View"

H

H (ruin)

H (ruin)

H

The Black Lane

O

O

H

O

H

O

H

H

Ballyknockan

Figure inscribed stone

*Map of village area by Matthew Stout (based on the Ordnance Survey by
permission of the Government, Permit No. 6529)*

Figure 2: Age and condition of houses in Ballyknockan 1997

	Occupied	Unocc	Ruined	Gone since '92
Pre-1838	12	3	6	1
1838-1908	15	2	5	2
Post-1908	8	4	0	1
Totals	35	9	11	4

Three buildings have an inscribed stone bearing a date, commemorating the original construction or perhaps a later rebuilding. Two are quite recent – 1920 (a forge) and 1933 (a farm building), but in the third case, the 'Land League House', the date of 1888 must represent a rebuilding as this house is drawn on the 1838 Ordnance Survey map. A fourth building had a datestone, the numbers on which are now illegible.

WALLING

The essence of Ballyknockan is the superb stonework. In most parts of Ireland, buildings are of fieldstone, roughly knocked into shape and distinctly functional. Here, building is taken to an art form. A few buildings are constructed throughout of very fine ashlar granitework. This consists of closely-fitting squared and dressed cutstone. However, at least forty-six surviving houses and twenty-two outbuildings have some architectural detailing in ashlar.

The chimneys of Ballyknockan are undoubtedly one of its chief glories and are an excellent advertisement for the skill and art of the stonecutters. They are of carefully-squared blocks, and fitted with precision. Other components which received particular attention are the surrounds of doors and windows. They are usually of superior quality to the rest of the walling. Eaves and copings (the stones forming the tops of the gables) are usually of cutstone.

Most of the walls of buildings are of coursed stonework. Few have had to be buttressed against cracks or settlement. The component stones have been carefully shaped and placed in position. Some of the larger buildings, including the 'Dancehall' and the quarry managers' houses, have ashlar facings.

Throughout the village there are cutstone pieces intended for houses and for public buildings in Dublin and elsewhere.

Well-built gable of an outbuilding: drawing by Margaret Keane

ROOFING

The vast majority of buildings in Ballyknockan have gabled roofs. This is in common with most upland districts in Ireland, but contrasts with neighbouring lowland Kildare. On traditional buildings, gabled roofs appear to be part of an architectural 'package' which includes stone walls and, in houses, a plan form called 'direct-entry' (see next chapter). However, a handful of houses have hipped roofs – these are a relatively recent introduction and are particularly associated with the quarry managers' houses, perhaps in imitation of the style of the higher-status houses of the landlords and their agents. About half of all outbuildings have lean-to roofs. The red 'Dutch' barns have the distinctive corrugated iron barrel roof.

Roof covering in Ballyknockan is dominated by slate, mainly old 'Blue Bangor', although recent re-roofings have tended to be in modern asbestos-cement slate. Until the early decades of the twentieth century, almost all houses and outbuildings in the Irish countryside were thatched. There is little evidence of thatch surviving today in the district – indeed the whole of Co. Wicklow has now only a dozen houses which have thatched roofs. Apart from

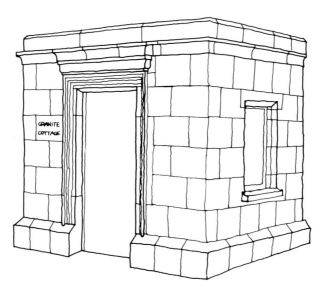

Porches and doors of houses: drawing by Margaret Keane

the occasional occurrence of rebates in gables to receive thatch and the roof timbering associated with it, the best survival of thatch is under the corrugated iron covering of one dwelling which is at present used as a byre. This roof is very typical of old vernacular roofs in upland and western districts. The timber structure is all roughly-hewn. The main structural support is provided by A-shaped 'couples' (heavy trusses) spaced 1.5 m (5') apart and braced by cross members about two-thirds the way up. Above these couples are rough, stout purlins at intervals of 50 cm (1'8") supporting a network of rough branches. Above these branches is a layer of thick grass sod. An oaten straw thatch is fixed into this sod layer with willow scollops (pins). The corrugated iron outer covering has been added at some stage since about the 1930s. The usual structure of slated and tiled roofs consists of A-shaped common rafters spaced 30cm (12") apart. Corrugated iron on its own is mainly found on outbuildings. A dozen houses, including some of the more recent State-built cottages, are tiled. About one-third of all buildings in Ballyknockan are roofless, having been abandoned to disuse and the elements, or occasionally converted into sheep pens or sheep dips.

WINDOWS AND DOORS

The surrounds of most door and window openings have received careful treatment. They are invariably of squared blocks and as stated above, a good number are of cutstone. The doorways and porches of some buildings, such as Granite House, the Ballyknockan Inn and the now-demolished Laurel Lodge are sumptuously-carved. Seán Rothery has described the 'astonishing doorcase' of Granite House as 'a builder's catalogue of tricks in granite' (Rothery 1997).

Windows are very often chamfered and the stones of their surrounds picked out in relief. The most familiar type of window in Ballyknockan is still the vertical 'up-down' timber sash. Most of the better-built houses would have had these windows from the time of their construction. Recent replacement of the sash window by uPVC, aluminium and timber casements has eroded the visual quality of a growing number of the old houses. This phenomenon is a serious problem throughout Ireland and, in a place of such great architectural and visual wealth as Ballyknockan, is particularly regrettable.

Pitching doors are to be seen in the upper front walls of some outbuildings. They allowed the pitching of hay up into the hayloft which overlay a ground floor stable or byre. These buildings have surprisingly good cutstone details.

Few original doors remain. The traditional half-door has disappeared and many houses have had porches added. An interesting feature of some houses is the drawbar, locally termed the 'dragging bar' or 'boult'. This is a wooden beam which sits in a long socket in the stonework at one side of the main door and at night was drawn across to fit into a smaller socket at the other side to bar the door against robbers.

House window: drawing by Margaret Keane

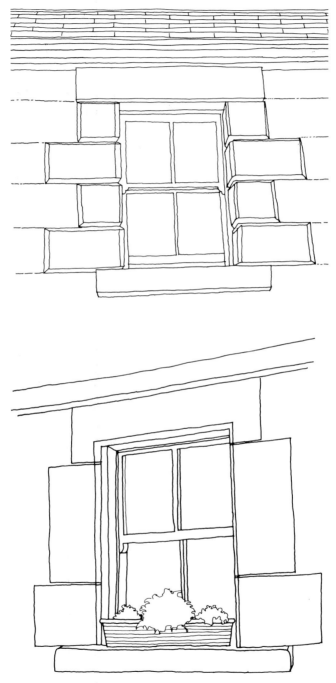

Windows of houses: drawing by Margaret Keane

Door of a building at the quarries

Pitching door at the first floor of a combined stable/barn

Drawing by Margaret Keane

FLOORING

It is likely that the typical flooring in Ballyknockan's houses was of stone flags. Hardly any now remains – the bulk has been lifted or have been concreted. Those which do survive are well-laid, rectangular flags. Originally bearing a roughish surface, they have been worn smooth by feet (especially where these houses were céilí houses) and furniture. Outbuildings tend to have rough cobbled floors rather than flags.

16

The Houses

Ireland's traditional (or vernacular) houses are generally of two types – direct-entry and lobby-entry. The *direct-entry house* is most characteristic of western and mountainous parts of Ireland. It is the typical Wicklow house. In these houses, the old kitchen hearth is located on a wall at the opposite end of the room to the front door of the house. The hearth may be situated on a cross wall or on a gable.

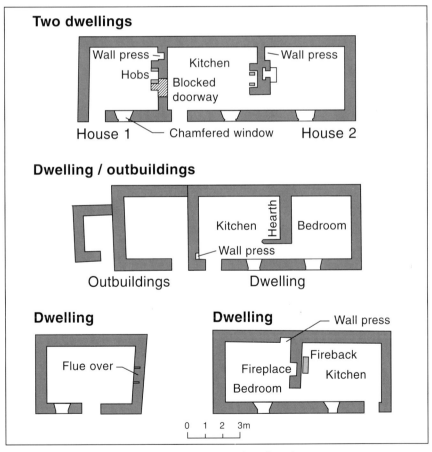

House plans (Matthew Stout)

Direct-entry houses are frequently built of stone and have gabled roofs (i.e. two roof slopes). *Lobby-entry houses* on the other hand are more common in lowland and eastern areas. The kitchen hearth in such buildings is located in line with the front door and is screened from unwelcome draughts by a partition wall (*jamb wall*). This wall is usually pierced by a small *spy* window, which permits a person seated at the fire to note the arrival of visitors. The small lobby formed between the jamb wall and the front door gives its name to this house type. It is the lack of such an obstacle to entry which distinguishes the other house type. Lobby-entry houses are very often clay-walled and hipped (i.e. having four roof slopes).

Almost all of the Ballyknockan houses are, not surprisingly of the direct-entry type. More curious are the three (built between 1838 and 1908) which are lobby-entry. It is possible that these houses were built by owners more familiar with lowland parts of Ireland.

HOUSE SIZE

The houses of Ballyknockan vary greatly in size. A sample of measured houses gives an average overall size of 11.9 m (39'8") by 4.55 m (15'2"). The average kitchen is 5.46 m (18'2") by 3.39 m (11'4") and the other rooms are usually smaller, with a length of 4.0 m (13'3"). Nine out of ten houses are two- or three-roomed, in equal measure and the rest are either one-roomed or have more than three rooms. Three in four houses are single-storeyed and one in five is two-storeyed; the others are single storey with a loft over one end. The two-storey houses are almost all post-1838 in date.

KITCHEN LAYOUT AND FURNITURE

The layout of kitchen furniture in the older houses conforms closely with tradition. Furniture is arranged along walls and doesn't impinge on the centre of the kitchen. The main items of traditional furniture are the dresser, settle bed, table and various types of benches (or 'forms'). The *dresser* was typically placed against the cross wall opposite the hearth. It was usually the largest item in old kitchens and stored all the family's crockery, cutlery and a range of other things, such as mementoes and receipts. The bottom part, now supplied with doors and containing pots and pans, was formerly open and occupied by hens. The *settle* is found along the rear wall of the kitchen to one side of and close to the hearth. This piece made a seat during the day, but could be opened out at night to provide an extra bed space, in keeping with the tradition throughout Ireland of having sleeping accommodation in the kitchen. Some settles have panelled backs and carved arm rests. Dressers and

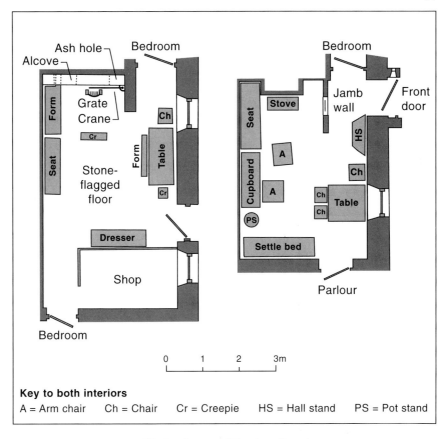

Kitchen layouts (Matthew Stout)

settles are now very rare in the district. Traditional rectangular wooden tables do survive and are always located along the front wall of the kitchen, under the window, where there was good daylight. An item which is now very rare, is the falling leaf table, usually positioned between the settle bed and the hearth. This piece of furniture was a space-saver – it could be fastened flat against the wall when not needed. Occasionally, there is a large food cupboard on the rear wall of the kitchen. *Forms* of many shapes and sizes can be found, mainly in and around the hearth and to a lesser extent at the kitchen table. The smaller, narrower, three- or four-legged *creepies*, are usually very rough pieces.

House in the centre of the village

Deserted house

'Hill View'

'Granite House'

County Council cottage

Ruined house in the centre of the village

HEARTH STYLES

All cooking and boiling was traditionally done at the kitchen fire. The simplest type of hearth is that in which the fire itself is made on the floor, typical for turf-burning, whereas coal is burned in a raised grate. One occupied house preserves the older form, together with its canopy of plastered timber or wattlework, supported on a stout timber beam (bressamer), spanning almost the full width of the kitchen. In other houses, there is a stone arch supporting the breastwork and the chimney. Many houses have well-built, often carved, cutstone firebacks and flanking arched or lintelled recesses, one of these being

Decorated fireplaces: drawing by Margaret Keane

used for storing fuel and the other, the bottom of which is below floor level, held ashes, swept in from the fire. The fixtures for the traditional iron or wooden crane survive in some houses – the cranes themselves are almost always gone. Iron ranges with cooking hobs, oven and water boiler have replaced the earlier arrangement in most houses, placed in front of the blocked-up hearth opening. More recently, modern bottled gas or electric cookers have taken hold and standard modern fireplaces inserted, thus ending the tradition of cooking on the hearth. In many ruined houses, only the flue remains, the stonework or wattlework of the hearth canopy having long disappeared. The traditional fuel of the area was turf harvested in Killough Bog, now submerged beneath the reservoir.

OTHER FEATURES OF HOUSES

The walls of traditional kitchens are usually adorned by family memorabilia and religious images and objects. Most prominent are framed prints of the Sacred Heart, Our Lady and occasionally some of the saints, as well as the current Pope and Padre Pio. Crucifixes, Sacred Heart lamps and holy water fonts and religious calendars are also common. Of a secular nature are photographs of family members and acknowledgments of academic, musical or

House chimney: drawing by Margaret Keane

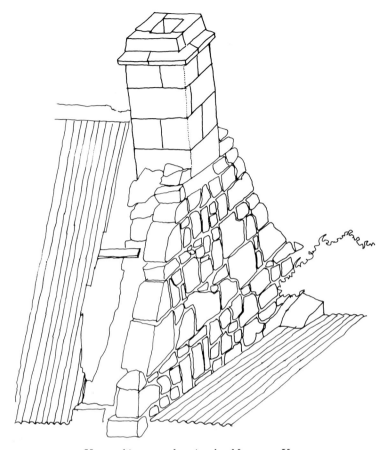

House chimneys: drawing by Margaret Keane

other achievements. Photographs of stone-cutting scenes also occur. Old mantle and wall clocks, Staffordshire dogs in china or chalk are also familiar.

Bedroom and parlour fireplaces are much smaller than those of the kitchen and often have metal or timber surrounds. Some are built in stone, crafted to a very high standard and decorated with geometric, scroll or floral motifs.

Parlour furniture tends to be similar to that found in any house of the period and less likely to have been the work of a local craftsman. These rooms were little used and occasionally accommodated a guest or received an important visitor. They had round tables, decorative lamps, a sideboard and firescreen in front of a fireplace with a metal or carved wooden fireplace, although some very finely-carved stone ones are also found. Parlours tend to have family photographs and prints of landscapes and historical personages and scenes.

Bedroom furniture comprises brass and canopied beds, wash stands, large heavy wardrobes and wooden or metal chests. Bedrooms are more likely to have religious pictures and crucifixes.

A local man stated that many houses formerly had a stone with an in-

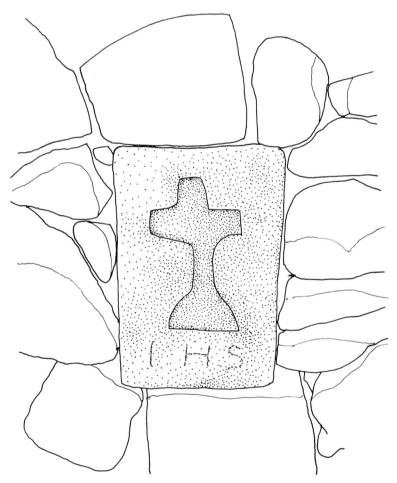

Stone with cross in low relief, from a house now destroyed: Margaret Keane

scribed or carved cross on it and set into one of the walls. This was done in order to protect the family, the house, their animals and possessions from misfortune. One of these, originally in a dwelling, now largely ruined, has been built into a boundary wall. It bears a cross carved out in low relief and has a pair of initials (the builder?) and an illegible date (the date of construction?).

17

Farmyards and field fences

FARMYARD TYPES

The layout of Irish farmyards changes from region to region. Variations on the courtyard theme are most common. Ballyknockan is no different, although the irregular topography has meant more irregular shapes of yard than one would find in flatter, lowland areas. A typical layout comprises a long rectangular yard formed by an L-shaped arrangement of buildings – the dwelling house with an outbuilding (byre or stable) attached and a second outbuilding detached and at right angles to the front of one end of the other range of buildings. The dwelling houses usually face the public road, with a low wall defining their road boundary and with a small yard or garden between the house and boundary wall. A small number of farmhouses present their backs to the road and face into their yards. The quarry managers' yards are substantial complexes with large detached dwellings facing the public road and having various outoffices, including a carthouse, to one side and to the rear. These properties are bounded by mortared walls. The traditional term 'street' can be used to describe a few farmyards, where there is a parallel arrangement, the dwelling house facing its outbuildings across a thoroughfare or right-of-way.

FARM BUILDINGS

The types of outbuildings found in the farmyards include byres, stables, barns, storage sheds, carthouses (latterly garages) and pig sties. There are a number of very big outbuildings which housed large items of machinery, such as threshing machines and vehicles. To each side of one or more doors can be found 'jostle stones', tapered stones which were placed in such a way as to prevent the hubs of cartwheels from damaging or dislodging stones from the doorways. One corner of some outbuildings has been chamfered or cut back for some of its height for the same reason. The building known as the 'Dancehall' or 'barn cinema' is two-storeyed to the front and one storey over basement at the rear. The lower floor was formerly a byre, the upper an extensive hayloft, access to which was by two sets of stone steps. Latterly, this building was used for entertainment – dancing and film-screening. Two-unit outbuildings, about two-thirds the length of the farmhouse are the norm, although a few single-unit calfhouses or stores are also found. Windows and

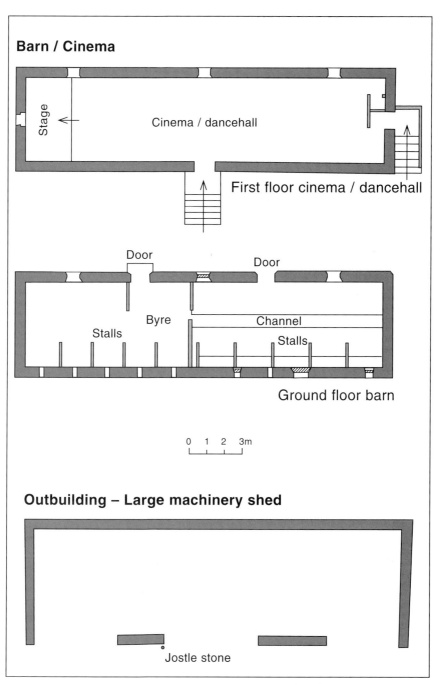

Plans of non-domestic buildings by Matthew Stout

doors of outbuildings are often treated in a similar fashion to the dwelling house and may also have decorative working.

In more isolated parts of Ballyknockan, small shelters may be seen. These are often incorporated into field walls and have lean-to roofs. They have a doorway but no windows.

Outbuildings

Outbuildings

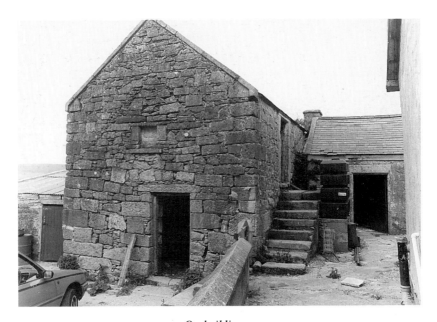

Outbuildings

FIELD FENCES AND THEIR FORMS

The field boundaries of County Wicklow are in general akin to those in any upland region in Ireland. The ubiquitous granite has ensured an abundance of material for the construction of field boundaries. It is clear that the process of wall-building satisfied the twin needs of keeping in animals and of providing a means of clearing away field stones or unused quarry blocks. These granite boundaries can also be termed *clearance walls*, a phenomenon known since the advent of animal husbandry in Ireland.

If one looks at the sides of the main road through Ballyknockan from Lacken and Valleymount, one sees a bewildering variety of wall types. Stone walls are so distinctive in the district that protecting them from damage or removal is of the utmost importance.

There are some impressive examples of *quarry-block walls* in Ballyknockan. The east side of the Horse Lane, as mentioned earlier, is a wall 2.55m (8'6") high and 1.85m (6') thick. On the Old Road, there is a huge clearance wall or cairn 30m (100') long, 3m (10') high and 4.5m (15') thick.

Boulder walls are composed of large field stones rather than quarried blocks. They are often supplemented by a hedge or trees.

Rough, uncoursed walls of irregular-sized stones are very common in Balyknockan townland.

Post-and-panel walls are very characteristic of the district. They are composed of rough irregular stones built to a height of about 1-1.5m (3'-5') and

Well-fitted wall in the village

Quarry-block wall on the Old Road

have 'scantlings' – narrow stone posts about 1.5m (5') high at intervals of about 4m (13') and perforated to take barbed wire. The panel of the name refers to the loose stones or blocks between the scantlings.

Well-built walls of tightly-fitting stones: These walls are an excellent example of utilising available resources to produce a structure which is at once useful and beautiful to look at. There is very little space between stones – each individual piece has been carefully selected and where necessary, dressed further for tighter fitting.

Mortared walls: The boundary walls of the quarry managers' houses are of well-coursed, mortared stone with well-made copings of cutstone, in contrast to the generality of field and boundary walls in Ballyknockan,

which are of drystone construction. The stonework is more consciously decorative and formal, reflecting the higher status of their owners within the village.

Earthen banks: Soil cover in the townland is in general very shallow. However, there is a system of earthen field banks in the low-lying marshy area at the Troman Brook. The banks are now only about 50 cm (1'8") high. Some are roughly faced with stone and all have drainage channels, formed after earth has been scooped out of them to form the banks running alongside.

GATEWAYS

Gates are so common a feature of the countryside that they are hardly even noticed. However, the combination of the forged ironwork of the gate itself and of the stonework of the flanking piers bears testimony to the skills of the blacksmith and the stonecutter.

There are many different forms of field gate, characterised by the style of their bracings. The most common form has four horizontal bars within a rectangular frame with two diagonal braces crossing at the centre of the gate in an 'X' shape. Gates with upside-down 'V' bracings are also very plentiful. Other gates have two smaller 'X' bracings or have parabola or arch shapes.

Smaller gates and gates into the yards of the larger houses tend to be more ornamental in character. They are usually two-part gates and may be painted silver or white. Many gates bear the name of the blacksmith or firm which forged or welded them. Some gates have a decorative scroll at the top of the slapping stile, i.e. the upright bar at the fastening end of the gate.

The **gate piers** in and around the village are often of very high quality. Twenty-one gateways have piers of cutstone. The simplest are tall, slender and square in section but for their pyramidal tops. Others are very large, with their corners chamfered, e.g. at the Ballyknockan Inn. The garden gate of Laurel Lodge has ashlared piers. Those at Rosie O'Reilly's house have exqui-

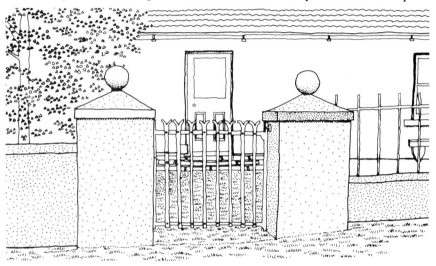

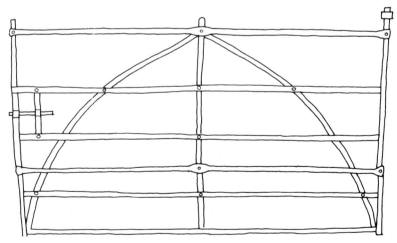

Gate and gateways: drawings by Margaret Keane

Gateway: drawing by Margaret Keane

sitely-carved caps, some topped by stone pineapples. Other piers have squat pyramidal caps topped by stone balls. Occasionally, gate piers bear the name of the property, e.g. 'Hill View' and 'Granite House'. Rougher gate piers are to be found accompanying field gates. They are usually tall and slender, sometimes tapered and rounded at the top and often still bear the marks of the wedges used to split them from the living rock.

Jostle stones, as mentioned above, are cut stones positioned to avoid damage by the hubs of cart wheels to gate piers or the corners of buildings.

They are often conical or tapered in shape, although others are low and dome-shaped. Two fine examples flank the main gate of Granite House and another two protect the curving wall at the junction of the main road through the village and the lower road towards the Ballyknockan Inn.

OTHER FARM FEATURES

Five **wells** and two **springs**, all but one of which is disused at present are marked on the large-scale Ordnance Survey maps (1908-1909). These were probably all communally-used water sources. This practice is recalled by the local names used to describe the small lanes which led to them – the 'Pump' and 'Spring Well Lane'. The spring at the side of the old Bog Road to Valleymount has an irregularly-shaped well-chamber which is built partly under the road. The most elaborate well consists of a well-chamber roofed with large stone lintels sloping downwards and a sill stone at the entrance. It is in the corner of a small rectangular enclosure built 50 cm (1'8") below ground level, which is reached by steps. Drains formed from carefully-fitted stones are visible in places where the road has been eroded. One crosses the main road trough the village and discharges down 'The Pump'.

Troughs of various shapes and sizes can be seen in some of the farm-yards and indeed in and close to the forges at the quarries. Some were used for watering animals and others for forge water, the red hot iron being plunged

Trough

Millstone

in for rapid cooling. Traditionally in Ireland, 'forge water' was regarding as having curative properties.

Cornstands or parts thereof can be observed in the district. They are essentially stone-built supports for haystacks. They consist of an arrangement of seven short standing stones, six making a circle around a centrally placed seventh stone. Termed 'staddle' or 'stackle' stones, they are tapered stones capped by a wide, flat, round padstone and stand about 60 cm (2') high. The projecting caps prevented rats from climbing up the stack. Wooden or stone lintels ('stretchers') spanned the gaps between the stones. A small crane was employed to lift the hay off a haycart ('bogey') and onto the platform. Most of the cornstands are collapsed and incomplete and staddles may be seen incorporated into the boundaries of some yards.

A few **sheepgaps** can be seen in the rougher stone walls. They are small openings at the base of a wall, which allow sheep, but not larger animals to move from one field to another.

Shepherds made use of **small huts or shelters** built into the boundaries of some of the more remote fields to provide shelter from the elements. Slighter remains of these structures are to be seen throughout the surrounding uplands.

Lintelled recesses built into boundary walls provided a convenient place for keeping tools or other items and occasionally, housed hens or ducks or perhaps a beeskep. These recesses are sometimes called 'keeping holes' or 'boles'.

Cornstand at Knocknadruse

Farm machinery

Scattered throughout the countryside are reminders of the immense importance of the horse in Irish farming. Horse-drawn machines of all kinds lie
rusting in ditches or sheds. In the village and its environs are several hay
(wheel) rakes, mowing machines, horse ploughs, potato diggers, rollers, pulpers
and farm carts.

Limekilns

These structures, which usually survive in greater numbers than the blacksmith's forge, are a reminder of the importance of lime to previous generations.
The limekiln was usually built close to an exploitable source of limestone.
This stone was crushed and then loaded into the kiln in layers, alternating
with layers of turf or wood. The large, circular opening at the top was closed
off, a fire lit at the base of the structure and the contents left to burn and
smoulder for a week. After this time, the limestone would have reduced to a
white powder and was raked out through the opening at the base. The lime
was then used to make mortar for buildings and walls, to make limewash, and
also as a fertiliser for the land (increasingly after about the year 1800). Clearly,
the all-pervasive granite at Ballyknockan meant that limestone had to be
brought in from neighbouring limestone districts. There was only one limekiln in the village itself, at the south end of the Old Road. Now demolished,

Limekiln, Carrigacurra townland

it was 2.5m (8') high and wide and had a small forecourt of the same dimensions to the front. The opening at the base of the kiln was roofed with large, sloping stone lintels. Limekilns survive in the neighbouring townlands of Carrigacurra – an excellent example at the west side of the road to Valleymount – and at the Lugnaskeagh farm cluster in Ballynastocken townland.

18

The quarries

THE GRANITE

The greyish-white granite of Ballyknockan has been described as follows
(Scott 1911):

> 'Works freely; fit for ornamental work. Much used in Dublin; Kingstown
> station. . . . Is one of the best known Irish granites for building pur-
> poses'.

The village of Ballyknockan exists because of the granite. Were it not for the
wisdom of the earliest entrepreneurs in identifying the quality and workabil-
ity of the stone and establishing the quarries, coupled with the skills of the
stonecutters who migrated to the place, there would be no stonecutting tradition and no Ballyknockan as we know it. Instead we are treated to the
consummate craftsmanship of many generations of the residents, exhibited
for all to see in the home village of the stonecutters and in the great public
buildings of Dublin City and elsewhere.

Granite exploitation continues today, but its main product is now ma-
chine-cut and polished stone for the external facing of modern buildings.
This is extracted from the main working quarry.

THE QUARRIES AND THEIR FEATURES

The quarries lie mainly to the east of the village. There are ten workings
altogether. Three of these, closest to the village proper, were in existence
before 1838 and include the present working quarry and two smaller abandoned openings to the south-west. All of the other workings are located in
lines running either south-west or south-east from the main quarry.

The large quarry is about 150m (500') N-S by 125m (400') E-W and
drops a sheer 20m (65') into a watery abyss. It has been described as 'a setting
of biblical grandeur waiting for Moses to descend with the ten command-
ments' (Williams 1994). A disused neighbouring quarry is about half these
dimensions and all the other workings are relatively modest, averaging about
20m in diameter. The smaller, disused quarry workings are worthy of conservation for historical and industrial archaeological reasons. Most of these contain
abandoned cranes and winches, workshops, forges, piles of quarried stone and

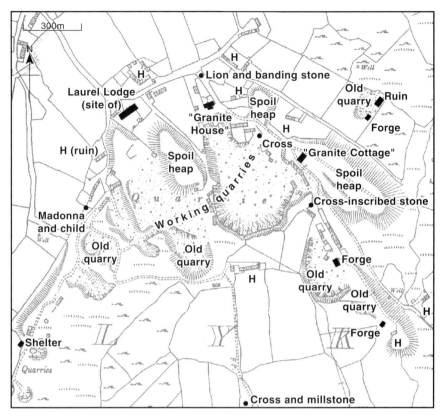

Map of the quarry area by Matthew Stout

great heaps of stone spoil. Some of the complexes contain worked and decorated pieces such as troughs, roughouts for crosses and architectural details
which were never delivered to their intended homes. Many workings have
returned to nature and support an abundance of wild flowers, especially the
foxglove.

There are many photographic records of the quarry workers – in particular posed shots showing quarry activity, the delivery of special pieces to
Dublin and the workers' own well-known Ballyknockan Brass and Reed Band.

Many of the buildings in the quarry zone of Ballyknockan are industrial,
including operational cutting sheds, disused forges and ruinous workshops.
There are also two large quarry managers' houses of especially fine craftsmanship and yards containing fine outbuildings and collections of worked pieces.
Outside of the quarry complexes there are a number of farmsteads and abandoned farm machinery.

Working quarry

Disused quarry

Crane in main working quarry

Quarry machinery

The most dramatic sight in Bally-knockan is surely the huge crane in the working quarry, perched at the highest point of the village and dominating all views of the district. It was brought here from the Dublin Docks. It was transported in three sections and reassembled at Creedon's quarry. It is a steel structure over 25m (85') high with a cab for the crane-driver. Abandoned cranes in the disused openings are very different in character. They are mainly built from timber with iron gearings and are about 5m (16') high. They comprise two upright posts which slant in upwards and connect at a pulley at the top. The movable arm of the structure is a wooden beam which is connected to the base of the

Older wooden crane in 'The Alley'

Abandoned crane made by Crendon's, Drogheda in 1873

Cutting assembly made by Anderson-Brice, Carnoustie

upright. Stretching from the outer end of the arm is a pair of rigid bars whose ends are connected to a pulley. This is held in mid-air by a cable which is fixed to the top of the upright post, runs under the pulley, passes over the pulley at the top of the upright and runs down and is coiled around a winch near the base of the upright. When the winch is operated, this causes the cable to loosen or tighten and so the arm of the crane moves up or down. The crane is held vertical by two wooden stays rooted in the ground and which meet the top of the upright. Iron tenons at the top and base of the upright allow the crane to rotate around these two fixed points.

The ironwork bears the names of the foundries. The crane lying flat on one of the large spoil heaps was made by T Crendon & Co Drogheda Iron-works in 1873. The mechanism of a crane standing intact in one of the disused quarries was made by Edgrest and Carr of Glasgow. Two of the five surviving old cranes are standing erect, the others lying on the ground. There are two old cutting assemblies in McEvoy's quarry. They are the products of The Anderson-Brice Co. Ltd Carnoustie and John Smith of W[?]eighly. Scattered throughout the quarry complexes are intact winches, parts of the structure of cranes, cogs and axles.

Quarrying and stonecutting tools

An enormous range of tools was used in the quarries. For extraction of the stone itself, there were plugs and feathers, crowbars and sledgehammers. Mallets, chisels and picks were used in stonecutting. In carrying out detailed work and moulding, masons' squares and lead templates were employed.

Forges

The six forge buildings are located in the quarry area and look like small, single-unit outbuildings. They are distinguished by having chimneys at one gable and have one standard door and a domestic-type window in their front wall. The quarry forges were used more for producing and tempering quarry tools such as sledges, plugs and feathers and crowbars, rather than for farrier work, i.e. replacing horseshoes. Forge hearths are open furnaces, the air for which was fed by large bellows made of leather on a timber skeleton. Latterly, electrical motors were used. Nearby is a trough for plunge-cooling molten iron and in the centre of the space, the anvil. This heavy block of iron had several perforations in it for mounting attachments used for shaping the metal in various ways. The work of the blacksmiths was absolutely critical to the success of the stone-quarrying and stone-cutting. Next to the 'Lion', to the front of Granite House, is a stone used for shaping the iron tyres of cart-wheels. A millstone at Granite House may also have been re-used for this purpose.

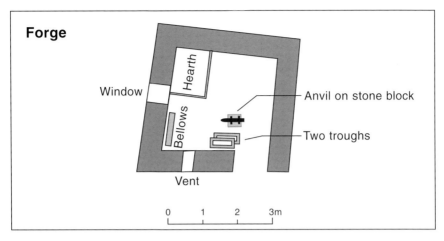

Quarry forge: plan by Matthew Scott

Workshops

In old photographs, the stonecutters are depicted working in or just outside lines of small sheds. Remains of these buildings survive at the quarries. They are lean-to, corrugated iron-roofed structures containing a number of compartments 3-3.5m (10-12') wide and 4-4.5m (13'-15') deep. In these spaces many stonecutters spent the bulk of their days and when a big contract required it, their nights. There are also some smaller shelters in the quarries.

NON-ARCHITECTURAL CARVED WORK

In addition to the great variety of structural pieces, many sculpted items were produced.

Crosses

Standing in a field due south of the main quarry is a cross about 1.4m (4'8") high, fitted into what appears to be a very worn millstone. The cross is said to have been erected as a protection against disease in farm animals. A fine, albeit unfinished Celtic cross stands inside the gate of the main quarry. It is 2.2m (7'4") high and is a worthy successor to the 12th-century St Mark's High Cross in the 'new' cemetery at Burgage, near Blessington. There are two cross bases with a recess in one face to take an inscription and also roughouts for two small crosses. One of these crosses is flawed, as its arms are unequal. More primitive is the boulder, at the side of the Old Road. It bears the inscription 'IHS' with a Roman cross over the 'H'.

Virgin and Child

Statues

Perhaps the most famous sculpture is the 'Virgin' which overlooks the lower village from its perch south-west of Laurel Lodge. It is a Madonna and Child and was not delivered as the Child is held in Our Lady's right arm rather than her left. A second such figure stands in a grotto in one of the quarry manager's gardens. Ballyknockan's most famous animal is the lion which failed to accompany the rest of the pride at the entrance avenue to Stormont, outside Belfast. It seems that the stonecutter misjudged the job, whittling the figure too much and not making proper provision for the finer carving intended to finish it off. At the opposite end of the sculptural scale is the crude human figure incised on a boulder at the lower end of the Spring Well Lane.

The Lion

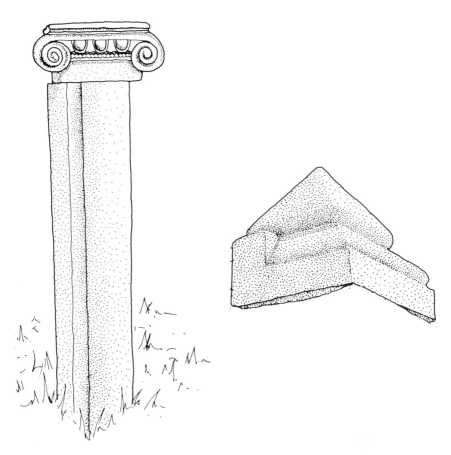

Undelivered architectural pieces: drawing by Margaret Keane

Miscellaneous items

There are two gravestones (one incomplete) inserted in a recent wall close to the 'Virgin'. One is dedicated to the Freemans, one of the old quarry families. The second, although more decorated, is uninscribed. In one of the small quarries there are roughouts for gravestones. In the surviving west gable of the 'Land League Cottage' on the Bog Road, can be seen the well-known plaque celebrating the rehousing of evicted tenants with the incription 'The Emergency Land-Grabber Defeated Here 1888. God Save Ireland'. At the various quarries are collections of architectural stonework never delivered to their intended destination. The most numerous of these pieces are finials for the pinnacles of gables and porches, urns, columns or parts of columns and pier caps.

Bullaun stone

The 'Ballyknockan Warthole' is probably the oldest example of stone carving in the district. It is a large erractic boulder about 190cm (6'4") diameter and 50cm (1'8") high with a cavity 20cm (8") deep and lies at the side of the Oghill Brook. It is in fact a 'bullaun stone' of Early Christian Period date (c. A.D. 500-1200) and may have originally been associated with ancient mining. According to local informants it was a curative well – pins were dropped into the cavity and the Hail Mary, Our Father and Ave Maria said. Other bullauns are associated with early ecclesiastical sites such as Glendalough and were used as holy water fonts or perhaps as mortars for grinding grain.

'Ballyknockan Warthole'

19

Conserving the village for the future

The importance and uniqueness of Ballyknockan to our national heritage is such that every step must be taken to ensure the integrity and survival of the historic fabric of the settlement. This includes the layout of roads, lanes and field paths, the disused quarry workings, the buildings and their contents, the sculptures and architectural pieces, the wells and the distinctive field walls.

Maintainance of this heritage

Vigilance is required to prevent the theft or sale of cutstone pieces from Ballyknockan. It is imperative that all items which are the product of the stonecutters remain in Ballyknockan.

It is important that the boundary walls which are such a distinctive feature of the townland and indeed of the district as a whole, be retained and kept in good condition. Often this involves nothing more than putting back in place those stones which have fallen. All drystone walls, whether of granite in Wicklow or limestone in Clare are prone to occasional collapse and there have always been expert drystone wall builders in such districts. It is necessary to retain and encourage the continuity of such skills.

The conservation of the older, disused quarry workings, together with their buildings, equipment and other items, should be central to protecting the industrial heritage of Ballyknockan.

New developments

These should take fully into account the historic context of their surroundings and should be of a very high design quality. In this regard, the fashion for applied 'crazy paving' to what are essentially concrete walls, should not be permitted. It is most inappropriate to ignore the skills of the stonecutting community which has lived and worked here for generations to resort to such poor walling techniques. New housing of the last few decades has generally ignored this historic context and the demolition of interesting and often finely-built structures to make way for these new developments has been to the obvious detriment of the village. The demolition, in April 1996, of Laurel Lodge, one of the finest and most important buildings at Ballyknockan and its replacement by a very poor facsimile has severely damaged a village which is supposedly listed for preservation. The lack of any consideration on the part of the local authority of the heritage implications of this demolition and of any referral of the matter to the statutory heritage agencies has worrying implications.

The Wicklow County Development Plan (1989), under the heading 'Villages or Buildings/Structures within villages listed for protection', lists 'Ballyknockan. Stone houses and items in quarry village'. The local authority's stated policy is 'that development does not detract from nor intrude on the setting of the structure, building, monument or feature . . .', that 'new developments will be required to maintain the quality and to respect the integrity of the historic setting . . .' and that 'particular attention will be given to applications for permission to alter or demolish listed buildings/ structures'. If these policies are actively and rigorously enforced, the future for the conservation of the historic, architectural and industrial heritage of Ballyknockan will be secure. However, recent experience has indicated that considerable vigilance is required by local people.

Successful conservation of the village will result if, (a) there is a broad local and regional consensus on the desirability of such conservation and (b) if detailed guidelines to achieve this are drawn up. The benefits of this course of action will include local and regional pride in what is an outstanding heritage and the safe handing on of this same heritage to the next generation.

Ballyknockan streetscape

Bibliography

Aalen, F.H.A.,1967 'Furnishings of Traditional Houses in the Wicklow Hills', *Ulster Folklife* 13, 61-68.

Aalen, F.H.A.,1994. 'Vernacular rural dwellings of the Wicklow Mountains', Hannigan, K. and Nolan, W. (eds), *Wicklow: History and Society*, Geography Publications, Dublin, pp 581-624.

Evans, E.E.,1978. *Mourne Country*, Dún Dealgan Press, Dundalk. 3rd rev. edn.

Griffin, Alice,1992. *Memories of the Liffey Valley*, Blessington Community Enterprise Group, Blessington.

Hannigan, K. and Nolan, W. (eds), *Wicklow: History and Society*, Geography Publications, Dublin, 1994.

Jackson, Patrick Wyse, 1993. *The Building Stones of Dublin*, Country House, Dublin.

Kelly, Martin J., (date uncertain). 'The Stone workers of Ballynocken [sic.]'. Source uncertain.

Lysaght, Patricia and Mac Gabhann, Fiachra, 1993. 'Rural Houses in the Poulaphouca Reservoir Area in 1939', *Sinsear* 7, 1-15. Murphy, Séamus. 1996. *Stone Mad*, Routledge and Kegan Paul London.

Ó Súilleabháin, Seán. 1976 'Beneath the Poulaphouca Reservoir', in Ó Danachair, C. (ed.), *Folk and Farm: Essays in Honour of A.T. Lucas*, pp 201-7. Royal Society of Antiquaries, Dublin.

Ryan, Nicholas. 1992. *Sparkling Granite*, An account of stone-cutting in south Co. Dublin. Privately published, Dublin.

Rothery, Seán. 1975. *Everyday Buildings of Ireland*, Department of Architecture, College of Technology, Bolton Street, Dublin.

Rothery, Seán. 1997. *A Field Guide to the Buildings of Ireland*, Illustrating the Smaller Buildings of Town and Countryside. Lilliput, Dublin.

Scott, Anthony, 1911. 'The Building Stones of Ireland', *The Irish Builder and Engineer*, 1911, 231-4, 306-7.

Valleymount Parish Newsletter, Various issues from 1990.

Williams, J., 1994. *Companion Guide to Architecture in Ireland*, 1837-1921, Irish Academic Press, Dublin, p. 387.

Index